Leading Change
TRAINING

Includes CD-ROM with Ready-to-Use Microsoft PowerPoint® Presentations

Exercises, Handouts, Assessments, and Tools to Help You:

✔ Create Effective Change Training for Executives, Leaders, Managers, and Staff

✔ Build Support and Reduce Resistance to Organizational Change

✔ Become a More Effective and Efficient Facilitator

✔ Ensure Training Is on Target and Gets Results

Linking People, Learning & Performance

Jeffrey Russell and Linda Russell

ASTD Press is an internationally renowned source of insightful and practical information on workplace learning and performance topics, including training basics, evaluation and return-on-investment (ROI), instructional systems development (ISD), e-learning, leadership, and career development.

Ordering information: Books published by ASTD Press can be purchased by visiting our website at store.astd.org or by calling 800.628.2783 or 703.683.8100.

Library of Congress Control Number: 2003102322

ISBN-10: 1-56286-319-3
ISBN-13: 978-1-56286-319-7

Acquisitions and Development Editor: Mark Morrow
Copyeditor: Rick Ludwick, UpperCase Publication Services, Ltd.
Interior Design and Production: Christine Cotting, UpperCase Publication Services, Ltd.
Cover Design: Charlene Osman
Cover Illustration: Todd Davidson

The ASTD Trainer's WorkShop Series is designed to be a practical, hands-on road map to help you quickly develop training in key business areas. Each book in the series offers all the exercises, handouts, assessments, structured experiences, and ready-to-use presentations needed to develop effective training sessions. In addition to easy-to-use icons, each book in the series includes a companion CD-ROM with PowerPoint presentations and electronic copies of all supporting material featured in the book.

Other books in the Trainer's WorkShop Series:

- *New Supervisor Training*
  John E. Jones and Chris W. Chen

- *Customer Service Training*
  Maxine Kamin

- *Coaching Training*
  Chris Chen

- *Leadership Training*
  Lou Russell

- *New Employee Orientation Training*
  Karen Lawson

- *Project Management Training*
  Bill Shackelford

- *Innovation Training*
  Ruth Ann Hattori and Joyce Wycoff

- *Sales Training*
  Jim Mikula

- *Communication Skills Training*
  Maureen Orey and Jenni Prisk

- *Diversity Training*
  Cris Wildermuth with Susan Gray

- *Strategic Planning Training*
  Jeffrey Russell and Linda Russell

C o n t e n t s

◆

We wrote *Leading Change* to help you succeed in moving your organization in a new direction, whether you are an organizational leader, consultant, or human resource or organizational development specialist. Our goal was to write a book that gives you insight, guidance, templates, and a flexible set of interactive training modules you could customize to fit a wide variety of organizations and situations.

The model and approaches for leading organizational change set forth in *Leading Change* emerged from our years of experience in consulting and training with a diverse clientele. The insights and lessons included here have been tested and found effective in our work with financial institutions, manufacturers, universities, medical institutions, state and local governments, multinational organizations, and even small mom-and-pop businesses.

The genesis of this book lies in some lively conversations with Mark Morrow, of the American Society for Training & Development. Mark recognized the need for a training workshop book about leading change and had confidence in our ability to write it. His support and commitment throughout the project kept us going.

The help we received from Rick Ludwick of UpperCase Publication Services, Ltd., who served as our editor, was invaluable. He rooted out our occasional lapses, inconsistencies, and errors, helping to improve our work and better serve your needs as a reader and trainer.

We also want to thank the many clients who have taught us what works and what doesn't in leading change, consulting, and training. Leading organizations through change is certainly more art than science, and our clients have given us an opportunity to polish our craft while enabling us to help them achieve their goals.

In the world of organizations, change comes with the territory. We hope this book will make navigating this territory a bit easier. Best of luck as you begin your journey at leading change in your organization!

Linda and Jeffrey Russell
Madison, Wisconsin
March 2003

Introduction: How to Use This Book Effectively

- Discussion of the value of an effective training and development program on leading change

- Comments on designing change workshops for executives, leaders, managers, and supervisors, as well as staff

- Explanation of how to use this workbook most effectively

- Description of what's included in this workbook and on the CD

Every organization is where it is today because of a multitude of changes. Whether these involved moving from a small "kitchen table" or garage-housed operation to a stand-alone business; doubling staff size over two years; embracing a new manufacturing process; adopting new technologies to serve customers; dealing with turnover in key positions; relocating operations to a different geographic location; focusing on a new customer base; or a host of other possible shifts in direction, focus, or operations, your organization's history is a chronology of the changes it has experienced.

Some of these changes have been joyful and others have been painful. Some have achieved their goals, while others have been complete failures at realizing their intended objectives. All of these changes, however, have left their mark on the organization and on those who were either leading the change or were affected by it. The goal of any change initiative is to achieve certain organizational strategic or operational objectives while minimizing the pain, disruption, and disequilibrium it can create for employees and customers.

Although the absence of change is death to the future of any organization (or at least obsolescence), the presence of change that is perceived as tumultuous and relentless can lead to organizational disintegration. Neither option (death by status quo or disintegrating change) is a particularly healthy place to be.

Effective change leaders, trainers, and organizational development consultants can avoid both of these unacceptable options by knowing how to provide others with a framework for leading change in their organizations.

The Value of an Effective Training Program on Leading Change

Building the skills of change leadership in your organization will have a tremendous impact on the results you achieve. The value of an effective training and development program on leading change will immediately be visible through your employees' better understanding of the reasons behind a change, lower levels of resistance to new ideas or approaches, a higher degree of initial commitment to the change, and a longer-lasting commitment to embracing change as a new approach for sustaining organizational success.

The evidence—and perhaps your own personal experience—suggests that the absence of a thoughtful and informed approach toward leading change leads to discouraging results. A survey conducted by Kepner-Tregoe found that for 11 different types of change initiatives (including productivity improvement, quality initiatives, cultural change programs, empowerment/involvement activities, and reengineering) only 20 percent of respondents indicated that these initiatives had met or exceeded expectations.

A study of 584 companies in the United States, Canada, Germany, and Japan, conducted by Ernst and Young and the American Quality Foundation, found that the majority of quality initiatives failed to achieve significant improvement. And, finally, in yet another study of executive perceptions by Kepner-Tregoe, nearly two out of three executives surveyed felt that employee morale was "worse" or "the same" as a result of change initiatives that had been undertaken by their organizations. More than 60 percent of these executives rated their employees' reactions to organizational change as neutral, skeptical, or actively resistant.

Fortunately, there is an alternative to these unfortunate results: a well-designed training and development program that integrates the insights gleaned from successful and unsuccessful change efforts with good instructional methods and technologies. A well-thought-out training program that is designed for a specific change initiative actually compels the organization to consider some fundamental questions before beginning a change initiative. It can also provide a roadmap to guide leaders and staff along the often treacherous path toward the goal of the change.

A training program that is closely aligned with a change effort can make all the difference as to whether the company hits or misses its mark. And, given the substantial direct and indirect costs of most change efforts, most organizations can't afford to get it wrong. Training's value lies in focusing the vision and goals for the change initiative, communicating expectations to key stakeholders in the change, and guiding people at all levels of the organization in helping themselves and others through the organizational and personal challenges presented by the change.

Designing Two Types of Training Programs

An important bonus of this book is that it offers change training designs and methods for two groups of participants: the executives, leaders, managers, and supervisors who are often the agents of change and the staff who are often directly affected by a change.

By explaining how to design training programs targeted to change leaders, this book helps the leaders understand their role within the change process, how to involve others in designing the change, how to deal with resistance when it occurs, and how to build employee commitment to new ideas or methods. The competencies of the change leader include both the skills of designing and introducing change and the skills of guiding others successfully through it.

By explaining how to develop training programs targeted to the employees who are directly affected by a proposed change, this book helps employees better understand the reasons behind a change, how to take a more proactive (and therefore healthy) role in influencing the design of a change, how to take care of themselves to avoid emotional and physical fallout from a change, and, finally, how to strengthen their own resilience in the face of difficult changes. The competencies to be developed in employees through these skill-building sessions include how to influence change for the better and how to take care of themselves throughout the change process.

How to Use This Workbook Most Effectively

Whether you are an experienced trainer or a novice instructor, you will find this workbook a useful resource for developing and facilitating change workshops for both leaders and those affected by a proposed change. By understanding the basic concepts about how change works and then reviewing the sample training program designs, you will be able to custom-design the program you need to offer a given audience.

If you have used the other books in the Trainer's WorkShop Series, you might notice that this book offers only single- or two-day options for training. Other books in the series, *Customer Service Training, New Supervisor Training,* and *New Employee Orientation,* offer scripted options for a half-day, full-day, or multi-day programs. This book is a little different. Because change does not happen in a vacuum and usually affects an organization from top to bottom, the programs in this workbook offer the minimum recommended amount of training for leaders, managers, and employees. You can use the material provided to meet your own needs, either by creating longer or shorter programs or by adding some of your own material. Keep in mind, however, that thoughtful training is key to successful change. It is difficult to rush the process.

To derive the greatest benefit from this book, the authors recommend that you follow these steps as you design your training program:

◆ **Skim the book.** Take a quick look through the entire contents of this workbook. Study the "What's in This Chapter?" lists. Get a good sense of the layout and structure of what's included.

◆ **Understand the mechanics and dynamics of change.** Read chapter 2 to gain important insights about change, how it affects people, and the critical role that both leaders and staff play in enabling change to finally provide positive results for the organization, its employees, its customers, and its investors.

◆ **Assess your organization's readiness for change.** Chapter 3 introduces a variety of methods, approaches, and tools for assessing the level of "change readiness" in both leaders and staff. The important message of this chapter is that you don't begin a change initiative without understanding the possible reactions that a variety of stakeholders are likely to have when confronted with the change. With a better understanding of your organization's readiness for change, your skill-building efforts are more likely to be successful because you will have customized your training to fit the readiness of your target audience.

◆ **Review the methods for good training design and creating a positive learning environment.** By reading chapter 4 you will review approaches and strategies for effectively teaching adults, preparing them for learning, supporting the "transfer" of knowledge to practice, and designing effective training programs. Even if you are an experienced trainer, you should find that a review of this chapter will reinforce what you are probably already doing—and perhaps add to your toolkit for effective instructional design.

◆ **Consider conducting an evaluation of your Leading Change Workshops.** Chapter 5 describes the levels of evaluation and suggests the strategies and alternatives you should explore prior to offering your training workshop.

◆ **Explore the training modules.** Chapters 6 through 8 offer a variety of training programs upon which you can draw as you design a program to fit your audience. From a two-hour executive briefing for change leaders to a day-and-a-half training program targeted to employees, you will see a number of training program designs that you can use as is or customize to your liking.

◆ **Design your training program.** With your target audience defined, the level of change readiness in your organization determined, your organization's change objectives clarified, and the learning modules contained in this workbook understood, you can design your own training program.

What's in This Workbook and on the CD?

All of the training instruments, tools, course handouts, and PowerPoint slides referred to in this workbook are included on the accompanying CD. Follow the instructions in the appendix "Using the Compact Disc" and the document from the CD titled "How to Use the Contents of the CD" to access the various documents on the disc.

The training materials in this book and CD include

◆ tools and strategies for assessing the change readiness of your organization (chapter 3)

◆ training workshops that can be used as is or modified in response to your organization, its challenges, and your own teaching style (chapters 6 through 8)

◆ learning activities that are designed to fit into the training modules (chapter 9 and CD)

- tools for facilitating training workshops and encouraging active learning, integration of content, and strengthened learning application back on the job (chapter 10 and CD)

- printable documents that can be used as workshop handouts (CD)

- Microsoft PowerPoint presentations and slides for your use in focusing the energy of workshop participants (CD)

- additional resources for future reference—including books and Websites that you may find helpful in designing effective training programs and in understanding change leadership.

Icons

For easy reference, icons are included in the margins throughout this workbook to help you quickly locate key elements in training design and instruction. Here are the icons and what they represent:

CD: Indicates materials included on the CD accompanying this workbook.

Clock: Indicates recommended timeframes for an activity.

Handout: Indicates handouts that you can print or copy from the CD and then use in ways that enhance the training experience.

Key Point: Alerts you to key points that should be emphasized in relation to a particular topic.

Learning Activities: Identifies learning activities included in chapter 9.

PowerPoint Item: Indicates PowerPoint presentations and slides that can be used jointly or individually. These presentations and slides are on the CD included with this workbook, and reference copies of the slides are included in chapters 6 through 8. Instructions for using PowerPoint slides and the CD are included in the appendix.

Tool: Identifies specific tools, checklists, and assessments that are used before, during, and following the training workshop.

Training Instrument: Identifies the interactive training activities.

What to Do Next: Highlights recommended actions that you can take to make the transition from one section of this workbook to the next or from a specific training activity to another within a training module.

What to Do Next

- ◆ Review the next chapter to better understand the origins of change in your organization and the mechanics involved in leading people through the emotional journey begun by introducing change.

- ◆ Consider the assumptions you have about change and its impact on people.

- ◆ Begin reflecting upon how the employees in your organization tend to respond to change initiatives.

◆ ◆ ◆

Before you begin designing your leading change workshop, it's best that you spend some time understanding the fundamental characteristics of change—and the assumptions about change made by the authors. The next chapter identifies the key internal and external forces causing change in organizations and introduces an integrative model for leading people through their emotional reactions to change. The chapter also identifies some of the actions leaders can take to help people move through change. The chapter ends with the underlying assumptions about change that influenced this book's content.

◆

How Organizational Change Affects Us

What's in This Chapter?

- ◆ The nature of change

- ◆ The forces for change

- ◆ The impact of change on people

- ◆ The role of leadership in the change process

- ◆ The governing assumptions behind the integrative change model for leading change

Recall from the last chapter the sad history of most major change initiatives. The results have been disappointing: wasted resources, low staff morale, marginal results, and missed opportunities. It's clear that there must be a better way—and there is. Although this "better way" has been with us for a long time, we have difficulty integrating what many of us know about change into our actual leadership strategies and practices. Leading change effectively is simple in concept, but quite difficult in practice.

So, how do we translate what are essentially simple ideas into practice? The answer begins with a thorough understanding of the nature of change, an exploration of the underlying forces that are causing the change, and a consideration of the impacts—emotional and physical—that organizational change has on people. It also includes a clear definition of the leader's role as a change agent, a change leader.

The Nature of Change

Change disrupts the status quo. It breaks the momentum and continuities that represent the steady streams of our lives and organizations. Change "shocks" us out of a comfortable place and moves us into discomfort. This is true even for change that we perceive as positive and useful.

The dictionary defines change as "to make the form, content, or future course of something different from what it is, or from what it would be if left alone" and "to transform or convert." In both definitions, the heart of change is movement, transition, and discontinuity. Although a given change may be necessary for survival, it still fundamentally tampers with something stable that has been carried along by momentum.

It is the nature or character of change, more than its definition, that concerns us here. When we are attempting to lead change in our organizations, we must understand its character, for when we understand its fundamental nature we are more likely to be better prepared for the inevitable challenges it creates for our organization—and for us.

There are two aspects of change's nature that profoundly influence the course of change in an organization and its impact on others (Russell, 1998).

1. Change and the forces for change introduce disruptions that can significantly diminish both the organization's and the individual's capacities to envision a clear and positive future. The more disruptive a change is to the status quo, the greater it diminishes the capacity to envision the future, and the more likely it is that it will have a negative effect upon personal and organizational self-confidence, competence, morale, and overall self-esteem.

2. The path of change is unpredictable. The leaders of change may think they know where the change will lead them, but there are *always* unintended consequences when you disrupt a stable system. You may get a lot more than you expected—and none of what you hoped.

Effective change leaders quickly realize that the change itself has to change in order to respond to emerging issues; customer and employee reactions; financial realities; pressing deadlines; and a host of other environmental, competitive, investment, and organizational pressures. In spite of a leader's efforts to think strategically and manage or control the change process, the path and destination of change is unknowable. Once initiated, change follows its own path, which means that people other than the change leader are able to influence its future. The leader's work, then, involves staying engaged with the change by providing ongoing direction and guidance and actively working to shape the change as it evolves.

The unpredictable nature of change also has a significant impact on employees. Just when employees think they understand an impending change and how it is likely to affect them, the path alters. The common result is anxiety, frustration, anger, and even a sense of having been betrayed by the organization and its leaders.

It's clear then, that a key challenge for change leaders is to recognize this inherent nature of change—its potential for disruption and its unknowability—and then to work with its nature rather than against it. Working with these characteristics of change will most likely reduce frustration and stress in the leader while increasing the chances for achieving intended results for the organization and its stakeholders.

The Forces for Change

Sir Isaac Newton said it best: Unless acted upon by an outside force, an object at rest tends to remain at rest and an object in motion tends to continue in motion in a straight line. This principle, Newton's first law of motion, suggests that any physical object tends to resist change unless pressure is exerted upon that object by a force. If the force is great enough to disrupt the momentum (rest or motion), the object is nudged—sometimes catapulted—from its position to something quite different.

To understand change, then, we must first understand its source. This involves exploring the forces that are putting pressure on a relatively stable system (our organization) to force it into becoming something other than what it is. Once we look at the forces pressuring our organization, we can see that there are two types, as depicted in table 2–1: forces external to the organiza-

Table 2–1
The Forces Driving Change

EXTERNAL FORCES	INTERNAL FORCES
Technology	Leadership and vision
Economy	Performance failures
Market niche	Workforce demographics
Human/social needs and values	Employee dissatisfaction
Government policies, laws, and regulations	New ideas

tion and forces internal to the organization (Russell, 1998). Let's take a closer look at external and internal forces in order to explore the source of the energy that drives organizational change.

EXTERNAL FORCES

External forces are factors that put pressure on an organization from the outside. The most common external forces for change include

- **Technology.** Technology is a key driver of change in most organizations today. It is a major cause, in part, because in recent years technology has developed the capacity to profoundly transform both the way work is done and nearly all of the core relationships important to the organization (such as those with customers, suppliers, investors, and employees).

- **Economy.** Economic growth or downturns and a stable or volatile marketplace put considerable pressure on an organization. When the economy is booming and customers are buying, the organization might take advantage of its cash reserves or extend a line of credit to branch out in new directions, take on new customers, build new facilities, or develop new products. In different circumstances, economic downturns can lead to changes in customer buying patterns, which may compel the organization to pull back on its commitments, product lines, staffing levels, capital improvements, or even close some or all of its operations. In either case, the economy as a force for change is always present—even in the public sector.

- **Market niche.** Often paired with the economy, this source of change influences an organization by asking a fundamental question: Are we still a player in the marketplace? Changing consumer preferences, globalization, mergers and acquisitions, and vertically integrated companies that pose direct competitive threats to multiple organizations will continue to significantly challenge the niche of every organization in the years ahead. In a world in which the Internet enables almost any organization to reach customers anywhere at any time—cutting across political and cultural barriers—preserving market niche is one of the greatest challenges facing today's organizations.

- **Human and social needs and values.** Over time, our society and culture experience profound shifts in what people say they need, believe, or value. These shifts, in turn, have a powerful effect on what people expect from their social institutions and the businesses from which they receive products and services.

◆ **Government policies, laws, and regulations.** Reacting, reflecting, responding, and sometimes leading the preferences of consumers (human and social needs as discussed above), government exerts a powerful driving force for most organizations. Whether these laws and regulations influence how organizations hire people, how they deal with waste from their production processes, how they are taxed, how they are audited, how they protect their workers, what they must pay people, how they deal with information they collect (privacy issues), or a host of other aspects of organizational life, government has a lot to say about how organizations function.

INTERNAL FORCES

The internal forces are factors and forces within the organization that put pressure on it, its employees, its leaders, and other stakeholders to move in a new direction. Although often the internal forces for change reflect what is happening on the outside (the external forces), internal forces can also represent insights and ideas that are independent of the external pressures for change. The most common internal forces causing change from within an organization include

◆ **Leadership and a vision of the possible.** Leadership is defined as "to go before or with, to show the way; to influence or induce" and "an act or instance of leading; guidance; direction." If leadership is to "show the way," then a key responsibility and challenge for leaders is to move people in a new direction. The executive levels of any organization have, as part of their responsibility, the duty to define the direction and desired outcomes for the organization. Offering new ideas and creating a shared vision is a key part of this direction setting.

◆ **Performance failures.** If the organization fails to achieve its goals in such key areas as profitability, growth, new customer acquisition, customer retention, staff retention, and market penetration, it needs to change something to achieve better results. There is nothing like a performance failure in a key area to get people's attention and to indicate the need for a change in thinking, direction, processes, or actions.

- **Workforce demographics.** The composition of our society and, therefore, the workforce, is undergoing significant change. By 2010, the U.S. Bureau of Labor Statistics predicts that 32.1 percent of the United States labor force will be composed of people of color, up from 18.2 percent in 1980. In 2000, 60.2 percent of women were active in the labor force (up from 57.5 percent in 1990 and 51.5 percent in 1980) and this percentage is expected to rise slightly to 61.2 percent by 2010. Along with demographic changes, the attitudes that employees have toward work, work/life balance, job rewards, career aspirations, and other workplace issues can also be expected to change. As these demographic changes in society are reflected in our workplaces, there will be considerable internal pressures to accommodate the new diversity in employee needs, expectations, and aspirations.

- **Employee dissatisfaction.** When employees are unhappy with their jobs or workplace they'll let you know. Whether they communicate their dissatisfaction through complaints, high turnover, lower productivity, grievances, or other expressions of conflict, unhappy employees find ways to let people know that things are not okay. Employee dissatisfaction with such workplace issues as organizational policies, procedures, leadership, direction, performance expectations, and new initiatives is often expressed as a strong desire for change.

- **New ideas.** Finally, innovative ideas that challenge the organizational status quo can come from anywhere, not just from the official "leaders" of the organization. Employees, acting on their own initiatives, can offer ideas and suggestions for changing any aspect of the way an organization functions. Healthy organizations encourage this kind of contribution to the company, but these new ideas can sometimes challenge deep-seated cultural traditions and practices that have evolved over time and that may reflect the influence of the organization's founders.

Any effort to understand and manage change must involve a deep assessment and understanding of the complex array of forces that are causing the change. Identifying these external and internal forces is one of the first steps that change leaders take when trying to introduce new ideas and directions.

Exploring the Emotional Impact of Change

When a change initiative falls apart, it is usually due to a failure of leaders to truly understand—and subsequently respond to and manage—the significant impact of the change. Effective change leaders recognize that a change of any size or shape has an emotional consequence for those asked to implement or live with it.

In recent years a number of researchers and organizational development authors have explored the effects of change on people. Beginning with Elizabeth Kübler-Ross' five-phased death-and-dying model (denial, anger, bargaining, depression, and acceptance), such authors as William Bridges (endings, neutral zone, new beginnings), Daryl R. Conner (stability, immobilization, denial, anger, bargaining, depression, testing, and acceptance), Flora/Elkind Associates (denial, resistance, exploration, and commitment), and Daniel Oestreich (comfort and control, shock and denial, chaos and confusion, facing a new reality, and adapting and learning), have tried to describe the emotional toll that change can have on people. Each has identified patterns in the human reactions to change that suggest a nearly universal response that follows a predictable emotional journey.

Figure 2–1 represents an integrated model that seeks to blend together both our own consulting work in organizational change and the common themes from these groundbreaking authors. Our model presents a simple, clearly defined sequence of the most common human responses to change.

As figure 2–1 indicates, when change is introduced into an organization there is a natural and inevitable emotional journey that people follow when confronted with the new ideas or approaches. Beginning with Comfort and Control and ending with Learning, Acceptance, and Commitment, this emotional roadmap helps us better understand the array of responses we see in others when they are confronted by change.

COMFORT AND CONTROL

Before a change is introduced a leader must first create a "felt need" for change. In this initial step toward introducing change, the leader confronts the emotional roadblocks of comfort, control, and a sense of complacency. In the first phase of their emotional journeys through change, people generally feel comfortable, safe, and in control of their work lives. There is order in their environment. They understand where they fit in and what's expected of them. Although they may even be dissatisfied with the status quo, it is at least

Figure 2–1
The Emotional Journey of Change

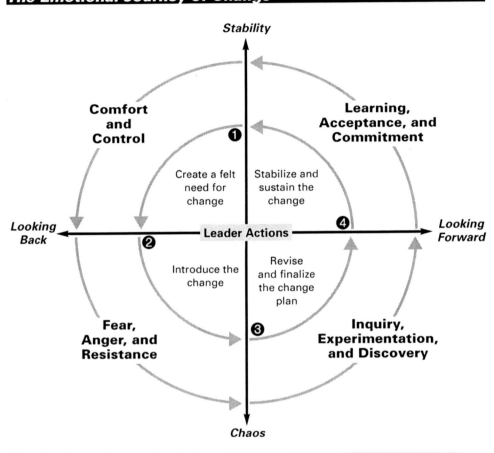

familiar to them; they have found a way to deal with the stresses of the world as it is. At this stage, the greatest challenge for the change leader is simply to get people to wake up! That's why the actions called for in this stage involve creating a shared feeling of need. The leader creates conditions in which people begin paying attention to the forces that are influencing the organization and its future success. For real change to take hold, people must first feel the need to change, the need to respond to forces that pose a threat to the organization's (and their own) long-term security, satisfaction, and health.

FEAR, ANGER, AND RESISTANCE

Unfortunately, experiencing the need for change immediately plunges employees into the next emotional phase: Fear, Anger, and Resistance. People feel anxious and uncertain—as well as angry and fearful—because what they knew to be true about the organization and their roles within it is being set aside. They have been told that the ways of the past and present are no longer adequate for the challenges of the future. Suddenly, the world is a more insecure and uncertain place.

How should leaders respond? Most importantly, change leaders must listen to and empathize with employees' anxieties and fears. A key action for leaders in this phase of the emotional journey is to offer specific solutions to the dilemmas ahead. In creating a felt need for change, the leader suggests that the status quo wasn't adequate for meeting the challenges ahead. By introducing ideas, approaches, and methods that solve these dilemmas, the leader is offering specific strategies for filling the void created by leaving past practices behind.

Another critical action for change leaders is to understand what employees believe they are likely to lose under the new rules and behaviors. Both anger and fear emerge when people perceive that, because of a change, they will be giving up too much of what they value and gaining too little. Fear that they will lose something important and anger that this is being taken away are natural and inevitable reactions. Leaders must acknowledge the perceived losses posed by change. They must listen to employee concerns, anxieties, fears, and doubts. And they must try to offset the perceived losses with the new benefits and opportunities that employees are likely to realize from change.

William Bridges, in his landmark book *Managing Transitions* (1991), writes about the endings that change creates for people. He suggests that acknowledging what has ended for people, what they are losing, and what they fear are essential leadership actions for this phase. With employee fears and anxieties reduced or at least buffered, the change leader can then begin shifting attention to the last of the emotions in this phase: resistance to new ideas.

Although, to the change leader, a given change is seen as solving the challenges ahead and an essential ingredient in the organization's future success, others are likely to see the change quite differently. Those who are asked to accept and implement the new methods or approaches may experience these as disruptive and threatening. Hence the emergence of resistance—the reluctance or even refusal by some employees to think, work, or act in a new way.

As with the other emotional responses to change, resistance is a natural and inevitable reaction when employees are asked to move in a new direction. Resistance is part of each person's cognitive autoimmune response: It tests a change to determine the level of perceived threat the change may represent. If the perceived threat is low, the person is more likely to work through his or her reservations and concerns and accept the change fairly quickly. But, if the change is perceived as a significant threat to the self and "business as usual," all of the person's systems can move into a "fight or flight" response. This is true even when we initiate a change that affects our own lives (for example, getting married). We are still likely to personally experience some level of internal resistance (for example, getting married is wonderful, but I'll be giving up my ability to make independent decisions).

The Sources of Resistance

People tend to resist change because

- they fear losing something that they value
- they lack trust in leaders or misunderstand their motives
- they disagree on the merits of the change
- they have a low personal tolerance for change.

© 1984, Randall B. Dunham, *Organizational Behavior* (Homewood, IL: Richard D. Irwin). Used with permission.

Effective change leaders recognize that some level of resistance goes with any change and take proactive steps to better understand and deal with its causes. As suggested in the sidebar here, these causes can range from perceived losses and disagreements on the merits of the ideas behind a change to a lack of trust in those leading the change to people having change-averse personalities. Successful leadership strategies in response to resistance involve communicating the vision behind the change; listening to people's concerns, anxieties, and fears; establishing a trusting relationship; offsetting perceived losses with gains; and inviting people to "co-create" the change's vision.

Involving others in helping to design the change itself accomplishes two of the change leader's primary objectives in the process: it tends to reduce employee resistance while, at the same time, actually refining and improving the intended change. When people are invited to help craft a change they make it better by bringing their practical, in-the-trenches perspectives to bear on the proposed ideas. This increases the likelihood that the "great idea" proposed by the leaders can actually be implemented at the frontline. And, by inviting resisters with concerns and complaints to suggest changes to the change itself, its design is not only strengthened, but also left with the designers' "fingerprints," thereby reducing the intensity of their autoimmune responses. It is harder to reject something wholesale that you've had a part in developing or designing.

INQUIRY, EXPERIMENTATION, AND DISCOVERY

As people's anxieties, fears, and perceived losses are listened to and addressed in the change process, and as they begin to take part in designing the change itself, people move from focusing on the past to focusing on the future. They choose, consciously or unconsciously, to begin making the change work for them personally and for the organization. This new phase in the emotional journey—Inquiry, Experimentation, and Discovery—is still an unstable and chaotic time, but one that is shifted toward the positive. In this phase, employees work to ensure that they experience positive outcomes by taking charge of how the organizational change plays out in their own work. They look for answers to such fundamental questions as where they are going, what they are expected to do, what they need to learn, and what rewards are involved. As they explore answers to these questions, they find increasing levels of clarity, stability, and focus. The chaos begins to subside, and along with it anxiety, fears, self-doubts, and uncertainties.

Leaders can be most helpful in this emotional phase by providing direction and support and by continuing to modify the change plan as new information and ideas emerge. When they help provide direction, leaders remind people of the vision behind the change, its long-term goal, and why achieving this remains important. When they provide support, leaders acknowledge continuing frustrations with the ambiguity of the change and with not having ready answers to important questions. Support involves giving people freedom to discover their own answers and to begin trying out these answers as they move forward. It also involves answering questions truthfully (saying what we know and what we don't know), providing frequent updates about progress, facilitating one-on-one and group discussions about issues surrounding the change, acknowledging people's hard work in helping make the change happen, and celebrating accomplishments along the way. Finally, by continuing to accommodate the insights and ideas of others into the change's vision and plan, the plan is likely to be strengthened and more readily accepted by others.

LEARNING, ACCEPTANCE, AND COMMITMENT

If the change leader can effectively manage the chaos, anxiety, and frustration of the preceding phase, people are more likely to move successfully into the last phase of their emotional journeys through change: Learning, Acceptance, and Commitment. In this phase people begin to see that the change—which has been tested, shaped, and molded by their own actions and the actions of others—is beginning to lead to tangible and positive results. They continue their searches for answers to the challenges posed by the forces for change and the change itself as they enter this phase. And the solutions they discover become integrated into their thoughts and behaviors. This learning, sparked by the chaos and confusion of the change process and the need to restore direction and stability, is the first sign of a real emotional commitment to the change. For the first time, people who may have initially resisted the proposed change begin realizing the promised opportunities and benefits.

The things that employees learned in Inquiry, Experimentation, and Discovery become integrated into an emerging definition of their new workplace roles, functions, and behaviors. They see other evidence that, despite how difficult the transition to a new way of work might have been, the change is starting to produce results that effectively respond to the internal or external challenges that precipitated it in the first place.

Leaders can be most helpful during this phase by encouraging and supporting employee learning and celebrating their successes and accomplishments. Celebrating the desired behaviors and rewarding the successes people are experiencing help reinforce people in taking actions that sustain the change. In this phase change leaders must also take steps to stabilize, reinforce, and sustain the desired behaviors to ensure that they continue. By building or strengthening organizational systems, structures, policies, and procedures that reflect the desired change, leaders can help ensure that the desired employee behaviors will be reinforced. These systems, structures, policies, and procedures include new methods for goal setting and performance management, reward systems that provide incentives for the desired behaviors, information systems that give people the information they need when they demonstrate the new behaviors, training programs that teach people the skills and knowledge required by the change, and the appropriate tools and equipment that people need to get their redesigned jobs done.

Although, ideally, the leader's efforts have helped guide people into and through the change to achieve the vision behind it and arrive at a better place, the relentless process of environmental challenge and organizational change continues. For just as the organization's leaders and employees sit back to enjoy the fruits of their hard labor and celebrate their accomplishments, people begin the gradual slide into the early stages of Comfort and Control.

Regaining stability in a better place—a place where the change process has led to significant improvements in the organization's health and effectiveness—is a good thing, but wise leaders recognize that there is danger in the comfort and complacency of organizational success. This is the paradox: Efforts that change leaders take to stabilize and reinforce the new ways of thinking and working may also reduce employee openness to new ideas, further improvements, or the next needed change. Effective organizational leaders understand that an organization that endures over the long term can never rest. So, although they must take action to stabilize the change and provide a place to help people reintegrate themselves in their new roles and functions, leaders must also work to sustain employee commitment to continuous learning and innovation and some measure of continued instability. There will always be a need for staff as well as leaders to identify and prepare themselves for the next change. And then the emotional journey begins again!

The emotional journey that this chapter has described is the heart of this book's content. Subsequent chapters and the training modules are designed around this model. Whether the audience is the chief executive and his or her leadership team as they try to introduce a change, a group of managers struggling to help their people through a change, or uncertain and angry staff members, this model will help you design and deliver a dynamic and effective change training program that gets results.

Governing Assumptions about Organizational Change

The change model introduced in this chapter and integrated throughout this book is based upon a number of fundamental governing assumptions. We want to make these assumptions explicit so you can better understand both the origin of the model and the training program designs.

Our assumptions about change and how to lead people through it successfully include

- **Change is inevitable; growth is optional.** Change is simply part of the human experience. It is ever-present and inescapable. You can't turn your back on change—it will happen regardless—but you can turn your back on growth and learning. And the absence of growth and learning leads to decline and obsolescence.

- **Change is difficult because it moves people out of their comfort zones.** When we're in the Comfort and Control phase, we feel pretty good. Change is like sitting on a tack: We have to stand up in spite of our desire to take it easy. Change introduces pain and movement as a path out of comfort, control, and complacency.

- **People don't resist change as much as they resist being changed.** There will always be some level of resistance to any change, but the more we involve people in a hands-on way to help define the change, the less they will work against it. When people design their own change, they recognize their own fingerprints. Their immune response systems say, "Hey, it's okay. I recognize part of me in this change."

◆ **Resistance to change occurs for a reason.** It emerges due to the lack of communication, the loss of something of value, mistrust of the motives or goals of change leaders, anxiety about an uncertain future, or disagreements over the design of the change.

◆ **People respond to change differently, based on their personalities, histories, personal visions, or perceptions of the surrounding environment.** The lesson from this assumption? Make room in your change process to help people move through change starting from wherever they are. Don't assume that everybody starts at the same place or moves at the same pace. In fact, some of your staff may be way ahead of you.

◆ **You can't change people; only they can make the choice to change.** You can, however, influence the choices people make.

◆ **The complexity and size of a change matters.** The more complex and expansive a change, the greater the level of potential disruption, the higher the level of likely resistance, and the greater the need for ongoing two-way communication. People desire continuity in their lives, and complex change often fundamentally alters both their senses of self and their hopes for the future.

◆ **You can never communicate too much during a difficult and complex change.** If people don't have information, they will make it up (and their version is usually far more Draconian than yours will ever be).

◆ **Resilience is important.** Those who do best in the face of change have the characteristic of resilience—the capacity to bounce back after a shock or setback. Effective leaders embody this attribute and help their people develop it.

◆ **Leaders don't control change; they guide, shape, and influence it.** Once initiated, change follows its own nonlinear path in response to uncertainties, reactions from the system, and guidance from the sidelines. The lesson? Rather than focusing their efforts on tightly controlling a change, leaders should instead focus on giving it order and structure and guiding the change as it evolves. Leaders should give direction, provide incentives, and give people the freedom to explore.

What to Do Next

- ◆ Begin thinking about the organizational environment in which you will be conducting the training.

- ◆ Review the next chapter to identify methods for gathering diverse perceptions of your organization, its leaders, and its employees.

- ◆ Begin developing some initial thoughts on the best approaches for reaching your target audience.

◆ ◆ ◆

The next chapter asks you to slow down and gather data about your organization's environment before you begin designing your change leadership training programs. You'll consider three methods for better understanding your organization's climate and the skills that you'll focus on developing in your training.

Assessing the Organization's Environment

What's in This Chapter?

- ◆ Assessment methods
- ◆ Assessing the cultural readiness for change
- ◆ Determining the core change leadership competencies to develop in change leaders and affected staff
- ◆ Assessing the degree of focus and clarity of the change initiative

Before kicking off your program to help both leaders and staff initiate and deal effectively with change, there are several critical pieces of the information puzzle that should first be in place. One of these is to gain a better understanding of the culture of your organization. Another is assessing the level of forethought that has gone into the change by those who are leading it. Yet another is to identify what competencies need to be developed in both those leading the change and those affected by it.

Assessing these issues—culture, change focus, and competencies—before you design and deliver a training program on change is a critical first step. Without a better understanding of these factors, your training is likely to miss the mark—or at least be less effective than it otherwise might be.

There are three approaches for gathering background information on your company's culture, change focus, and competencies: interviews, focus groups, and written surveys.

Structured Interviews

One-on-one interviews provide an opportunity to explore an issue in depth through a series of structured questions. The interviews should be structured so that the same questions are asked of all participants. You should pull a sample of people who represent a broad cross-section of your organization. Ideally, this should include representatives from the executive leadership, managers and frontline supervisors, and staff from different work areas. Each interview should last no more than an hour and should provide an opportunity for participants to offer their thoughts both in response to your questions and on their own initiative (in the context of the interview's focus). Following the interviews, you should summarize the results by noting the key themes and trends that came to the surface during your discussions.

Focus Groups

The wonderful thing about focus groups is that they provide an opportunity for you to explore issues surrounding change in an interactive way with each group. In response to your questions, you can facilitate the group's reactions to each other's comments and move beyond your initial questions to explore their ideas, concerns, and solutions. The goal of using focus groups is more to identify diverse perspectives and issues than to develop consensus around a given issue or proposal. The interactivity within the group and the opportunity to explore the issues in greater depth are the strongest selling points for using focus groups as a source of information. As with the interviews, you should draw the participants from a diverse cross-section of your organization. Whether you create homogeneous (similar in kind) or heterogeneous (diverse and dissimilar in kind) groups, each group should be asked the same set of core questions, with the opportunity for deeper exploration as necessary. Your goal in analyzing the focus group data is, again, to look for and highlight the broad trends in what people are saying.

Written Surveys

The written survey (whether distributed and completed online or on paper) provides a fast and relatively inexpensive way to gather information from a large number of staff. As with the other forms of gathering information identified in this chapter, you should ensure that you have sampled a diverse cross-section of your organization. This increases your confidence that you can generalize your findings to the entire organization. Although the written survey is the most effective approach for reaching the greatest number of people, it suffers because it doesn't allow you to interact with the respondents. It isn't easy to ask a follow-up or clarifying question or to explore additional ideas contained in people's responses. Although developing a written survey can sometimes be intimidating because of the need to ensure that the questions truly measure what you intend to measure, it isn't difficult to develop good questions that bring you closer to understanding employee attitudes and perceptions. Keep in mind that you are simply gathering additional information—even subjective information—to give you insight into employees' perceptions about change and the organization.

For each of these forms of data gathering, the quality of the questions, the diversity and distribution of the sample of people you involve, and how you analyze the data determine the actual quality and usefulness of the data. We recommend that you use all three approaches in your research, but you will need to select your approach based upon what information you want to collect, how much interaction you want with the participants, the importance of gathering information from as many people as possible, and how much time and how many resources are available.

Questions to Explore in Your Research

The questions you decide to explore depend upon the focus of your training and how much information you believe you need as part of your program design and delivery. The questions that follow, organized by the area explored, can be modified depending on the method you use for data collection.

ASSESSING THE ORGANIZATIONAL CLIMATE AND CULTURE

This aspect of the organization can be explored using any of the three information-gathering methods. Some possible questions include the following:

- What do you see as the major challenges facing this organization over the next five years?

- What are the likely consequences if we don't effectively respond to these challenges?

- On a 10-point scale (with 1 equaling not at all and 10 equaling quite a bit), indicate your level of agreement with each of the following statements:

  - ☐ Employees in this organization are quickly able to adjust to changes.

☐ The environment in this organization is one in which tradition and the status quo define how people work.

☐ When things get stressful here, people tend to help each other (as opposed to only helping themselves).

☐ The organization's leadership has done a good job of communicating during past changes.

☐ When employees have questions about a proposed organizational change, they are encouraged to ask them.

☐ The employees of this organization are accustomed to making decisions on their own.

☐ Employees are encouraged to share their ideas about how to improve the quality of worklife.

☐ In this organization, we tend to focus on blaming rather than exploring the causes of problems.

☐ In this organization, employees tend to be intimidated by those who have power.

◆ In general, are you wary of changes that the organization proposes in the way we work, make decisions, or manage information? Why or why not?

◆ What, if any, concerns do you have about how this organization has introduced changes in the past?

◆ How could the leaders here most improve their ability to lead employees successfully through change?

◆ To what extent do employees demonstrate leadership in their daily work? Give examples.

◆ The best way to reduce employee resistance and increase their commitment to proposed changes here includes. . . .

ASSESSING LEADERSHIP AND EMPLOYEE COMPETENCIES

Leadership and employee competencies are best assessed through focus groups and written surveys. Possible questions include the following:

- What skills and knowledge should our organization's leaders develop to enable them to more effectively lead the organization into the future?

- What skills and knowledge should employees develop to enable them to more effectively deal with the changes facing the organization in the years ahead?

- On a 10-point scale (with 1 equaling not at all and 10 equaling quite a bit), indicate your level of agreement with each of the following statements. This organization's leadership is skilled in

  - ☐ selling the importance and need for making changes in the way the organization does business

  - ☐ encouraging employee participation in designing the way we work

  - ☐ encouraging employee participation in decision-making

  - ☐ listening to employee ideas and concerns

  - ☐ responding to employee issues and concerns about changes in organizational direction, policies, procedures, and practices.

- On a 10-point scale (with 1 equaling not at all and 10 equaling quite a bit), indicate your level of agreement with each of the following statements. This organization's employees are skilled in

  - ☐ asking clarifying questions about a coming change

  - ☐ seeing the "big picture" of the organization and its future (as opposed to focusing only on their own jobs or worklives)

  - ☐ sharing their ideas for ways of improving the organization, its systems, and processes

  - ☐ constructively resolving conflict between individuals and work groups.

- What are the best methods for developing or strengthening the skills and knowledge you have identified?

ASSESSING THE CLARITY OF THE CHANGE'S CAUSES AND EFFECTS

These questions should be directed at those who are initiating change and are best done through interviews or a meeting with the change leadership team. Possible questions include the following:

- What are the factors that are causing this change to be made at this time?

- What are the consequences if we don't adequately respond to these challenges?

- What do you see as the final result (the change vision) once the proposed change is accomplished?

- How fixed or defined is this vision of the change? Will there be opportunities to adjust or modify it or how to achieve it? If so, when and how will this occur?

- What objections do you expect to hear from others? What experience suggests that you're likely to hear these objections?

- Who are likely to be the biggest naysayers once they hear about the details of this change? How do you plan to identify and respond to their concerns?

- What are the benefits that you see the change creating for those who help make it happen?

- What is likely to go wrong with this proposed change? Why? How do you plan to prevent this from happening?

- Once the proposed change is implemented, what organizational systems and processes (for example, performance management, information systems, reward systems, customer relationship management systems) will help reinforce the new behaviors expected of employees?

- To what extent does the proposed change conflict with the organization's existing culture? What actions are you prepared to take to help "sell" this change to a resistant culture?

- What is your plan for communicating the change and for keeping employees updated on the progress and adjustments the organization is experiencing?

Regardless of your data collection methods, you will find exploring the answers to these questions essential as you prepare your training program. Having insights from the data will help you prepare for the possible concerns and questions that may arise during the training. You can also design your training program with these factors in mind.

What to Do Next

- ◆ Develop strategies for gathering data on employee perceptions of the organization to help you develop knowledge and insight about the change.

- ◆ Work closely with the team of leaders that is initiating the change to ensure that they can use the data you gather and that it can be integrated into your training program.

- ◆ Review the next chapter to learn how to design and facilitate dynamic training programs that provide opportunities for participants to raise, discuss, and address key issues around the issue of organizational change.

◆ ◆ ◆

Once you have assessed the organizational climate, the key competencies you'll develop in both leaders and staff, and the clarity of the change's causes and effects, you're ready to begin designing your change training program.

Turning People On to Learning

- The fundamentals of adult learning
- Supporting the transfer of training
- Designing effective training programs
- Keys to effective facilitation

Training doesn't ensure that learning occurs, but it is a powerful tool for developing the critical competencies needed to meet the challenges facing any organization. This chapter offers some key insights into how people learn best, which will enable you to design training programs that actively engage people in their own learning and growth. This in turn will enable them to successfully do their work, make decisions, solve problems, and contribute to creating great results for the customer.

The Fundamentals of Adult Learning

There is a discipline for teaching adults new information, knowledge, or skills. Although learning has always been a part of the human experience—sometimes through necessity as much as desire or aspiration—some broad principles for guiding and facilitating adult learning have emerged over the past 40 years. Drawn from the work of Knowles, Brookfield, and others, these core principles, along with implications and suggestions for the learning and teaching environment, are outlined in table 4–1 (on the next three pages).

Supporting the Transfer of Training

The goal of training involves more than simply teaching essential skills and knowledge to participants. It also involves ensuring that what is learned in

Table 4–1
Key Principles of Adult Learning and Their Implications for Teaching/Training Design

ADULT LEARNING PRINCIPLE	IMPLICATION FOR TEACHING/TRAINING DESIGN
• Adults bring life experience and knowledge to the learning environment. The experience and knowledge include work-related, family, and community events and circumstances. • Adults learn best when they can relate new knowledge and information with previously learned knowledge, information, and experiences.	• Provide opportunities for learners to reflect upon and share their existing knowledge and experience. • Learning activities should be created that involve the use of past experience or knowledge. • Ask learners to identify the similarities and differences between what they are learning and what they already know.
• Adults tend to prefer self-directed, autonomous learning —but this is often not an expectation of educational institutions and society.	• Training should be designed around participants' needs and goals. • Ask participants what they want to learn. Learners learn best when they establish a specific learning objective or goal for themselves. • Provide learners with action planning tools and templates to help develop and focus their self-directed efforts and to facilitate learning. • Provide opportunities for learners to direct their own learning through guided inquiry and self-facilitated small group discussions.
• Adults have self-pride and desire respect. They need their experience, beliefs, knowledge, questions, and ideas acknowledged as important.	• Learning involves risk and the possibility of failure. Training should be designed to minimize each learner's risk and embarrassment. • Provide opportunities for learners to share ideas, questions, opinions, experiences, or concerns, and create an environment that honors and respects everything that is appropriately shared. • Create flexible training programs that honor participants by accommodating their contributions and questions as much as possible. • Make it safe for learners to express their confusion, anxieties, doubts, and fears.

	• Provide opportunities for "small wins" and little victories in the learning process—to build competencies incrementally.
• Adults want practical, goal-oriented, and problem-centered learning that can immediately help them deal with life's challenges.	• Ask learners to identify what they would like to learn about a topic. • Establish clear learning objectives that make the connection between participant's needs and the learning content. • Share examples and stories that relate the learning content to participant's current challenges. Ask learners to share their own examples that make this linkage. • Engage learners in identifying the challenges they face and the value of learning to addressing these challenges. • Follow theories with practical examples and applications to demonstrate the relevance of the learning.
• Adults desire feedback on the progress they are making at learning something new.	• Provide opportunities for learners to get immediate feedback to their own learning through case examples, role-playing, quizzes, and responses to trainer questions. • Encourage learners to assess their own learning and performance. • Praise any level of learning improvement and encourage continued learning.
• Adults have preferences for the way in which they learn. Some prefer learning by doing (kinesthetic), others prefer learning by observing (visual), while still others prefer learning by listening (auditory).	• Recognize that not all learners will respond to a given teaching method or technique. • Training delivery should involve a wide variety of methods that tap into all learner preferences. • Use all three learning modes (kinesthetic, visual, and auditory) in every 20-minute teaching interval. • Trainers must be aware of their own learning preferences and be wary of favoring this approach in their own teaching. • Small group work, dyadic discussions, and individual activities free learners to learn in the style that best suits them.
• Adults learn best through collaboration and reciprocity—an environment where people learn with others while sharing what they already know.	• Small group work and dyadic discussions provide a low-risk environment for learning while capitalizing on the different levels of knowledge or skill within a group. • Learner self-esteem is strengthened through team-based learning founded upon mutual trust and respect. • Small group learning more accurately reflects participants' interdependent and collaborative work environment back on the job.

continued on next page

Table 4–1, continued

Key Principles of Adult Learning and Their Implications for Teaching/Training Design

ADULT LEARNING PRINCIPLE	IMPLICATION FOR TEACHING/TRAINING DESIGN
• Adults are motivated to learn by a wide variety of factors. The most common of these include personal aspirations, externally imposed expectations, internal desire/interest, escape from a situation (boredom or fear), growth and advancement, and service to others.	• Inquire into the reasons participants are interested in learning. • Invite learners to identify the link between learning and the satisfaction of a personal need or a reduction in an external stress or threat. • Make a connection between the learning content and each learner's long-range objectives (in work and life). • Ask participants to discuss in dyads and small groups the short- and long-term benefits of learning the program's content.

the workshop is "transferred" to the workplace. The transfer of training should be of the utmost importance to the trainer because if a trainee learns what is desired but is unable or unwilling to apply this new learning back on the job, the trainer's time and the organization's resources have been squandered. For this reason, the "transfer problem" has been the focus of considerable debate and research.

In their book *Transfer of Training,* Mary Broad and John Newstrom (1992) offer a powerful model for better understanding and influencing the transfer of training. They designed and tested a transfer of training matrix that combines the three key roles involved in the learning experience (trainee, trainer, and manager) and the three time phases associated with training delivery (before, during, and after). The results of their research offer some important insights into the best roles and the times to support the maximum transfer of learning to the workplace.

As shown in table 4–2, their research revealed that the most powerful influence on the effective transfer of training from the workshop to the workplace is the manager's support for the learning prior to the training event. The second most powerful role and time period is the trainer taking steps to prepare the trainee prior to the training event. And the third most powerful impact on effective transfer was found to be the manager supporting and reinforcing learning following the skill training.

Broad and Newstrom's research, which was based on interviews with expert trainers, suggests that ensuring that both the manager and the trainer are doing the right things at the right time will provide the maximum benefit. Here are a few suggestions for reinforcing the transfer of training before, during, and after the training session.

Table 4–2
Perceptions of Most Powerful Role/Time Combinations for Using Transfer of Training

	BEFORE	DURING	AFTER
Manager	1	8	3
Trainer	2	4	9
Learner	7	5	6

Key: 1 = high effectiveness/potency; 9 = low effectiveness/potency.
Source: Broad and Newstrom, 1992, p. 54.

BEFORE THE TRAINING SESSION

Managers and supervisors can support the transfer of training before the training session by

- discussing the importance and benefit of the skills that will be learned in the training session to the trainee, his or her own work products, and the broader performance of the work area or team

- involving the trainee in developing the learning goals and objectives for the session in order to help the trainee understand the benefits

- supporting the employee's participation by providing assistance or backup for covering workload

- ensuring that this is the right person for the training at the right time (There's no point in sending someone who doesn't need the training or sending someone who does but who may be working under distracting pressures.)

- attending the training program in advance of the trainee or attending with the trainee

- developing a learning contract with the employee to reinforce learning goals and the value of skill acquisition

- sending the trainee to the session with others to facilitate and reinforce team learning.

Trainers can facilitate the transfer of training in advance of the training session by

- ensuring that the training objectives match the skill requirements of the organization, department, and individual participants

- sending a communication to trainees highlighting the program's goals and the session's relevance to their work and the challenges they face

- requesting that training participants complete pre-session work, conduct research, or complete readings.

DURING THE TRAINING SESSION

During the training session, the trainer's responsibilities for facilitating the transfer of training include following the principles of adult learning and ensuring that the seminar content and instruction relate directly to the participant's workplace. Some specific activities during training that facilitate transfer are

- asking participants to develop specific learning objectives for the skill or knowledge area

- providing cases, scenarios, and role-plays based upon participant examples and situations

- selling the on-the-job benefits of learning

- providing "job aids" that trainees can use back on the job and that aid learning and application

- facilitating action planning to guide training participants in developing specific "next step" application goals following the training session.

FOLLOWING THE TRAINING SESSION

Managers and supervisors can support the transfer of training following the delivery of training by

- meeting with the trainee to discuss what he or she learned and how he or she will use and apply the learning to their work or behaviors

- providing opportunities for the trainee to practice the new skills and behaviors

- giving positive reinforcement to the trainee when he or she observes the person practicing the learned behaviors or skills

- establishing a formal "debriefing" following the training to provide feedback and additional learning to help sustain the new practices

- granting an opportunity to practice the new skills.

The trainer can facilitate and support the transfer of training following the training session by

- following up with the trainee to check for understanding, questions, and progress in using the new practices or skills

- conducting refresher mini-sessions or discussions at specific intervals to sustain learning and application and provide opportunities for additional feedback and reinforcement

> ◆ being available to answer participants' questions and provide additional direction.

Simply honoring the principles of adult learning and taking the right actions to facilitate the transfer of training will be enormously helpful in the design of the training program. Before we move on to the change training modules, we want to offer some additional tips that will further help you in building and delivering a dynamic and effective change training program.

Designing Effective Training Programs

Training program design is more art than science in that a perfectly designed training program with all of the right content will fall flat if it doesn't make room for both the participants' learning preferences and the teaching style of the trainer. The program should reflect both the suggested content and modules in this book and your own personal style and approach to learning and teaching. Within this approach, here are some specific suggestions for effective training program design:

◆ Ensure that you do a thoughtful needs analysis of the organization and prospective learners before designing and delivering the training.

◆ Stay flexible in your design and delivery. If you need to change gears in response to what you're seeing or hearing, don't be afraid to do so. This means, however, that you must go into the session with significant depth in content knowledge. Be prepared.

◆ Actively involve participants in their own learning. Use a variety of interactive training methods: small groups, dyads, role-plays, action planning, pop quizzes, practice time, brainstorming, games, or guided inquiry are some common methods. Be adventurous and take some risks to help make learning happen.

◆ Break up the allotted training time into segments, with each focusing on a specific learning outcome.

◆ Design each learning segment with a clear beginning, middle, and end, and ensure that the training methods and activities you use support achieving the specific learning objective of each segment.

◆ At the beginning of the session give trainees the "big picture" of the topic and the issues you'll be exploring with them during the program.

◆ Solicit participants' questions and integrate a process of addressing these questions into your training delivery.

◆ Provide sufficient time for learning integration. Pace your learning objectives and supporting activities to allow time for trainees to reflect upon their learning insights and integrate them into their future practice.

◆ Provide supplemental worksheets to facilitate the trainees' recording of key learning insights (Ah Ha's!) gleaned from session discussions and applications.

◆ Build trainee action planning into your training program. Action planning helps build trainee commitment to applying what he or she is learning to the real world beyond the training session.

◆ End your training session with a recap of the key learning points and a final restatement of the value of translating the insights gained into daily practice.

Facilitating Versus Teaching

Facilitating trainee learning involves more than simply teaching or instructing participants. Facilitation includes creating and managing an environment that makes learning easy. In his book *The Skilled Facilitator,* Roger Schwarz (1994) suggests that the facilitator's role is to help groups and individuals improve through "valid information, free and informed choice, and internal commitment to the choices." Schwarz suggests that a fundamental characteristic of the facilitator is to invite the trainee into a learning opportunity in which the trainee has maximum choice as to whether and how he or she will learn. With these conditions of information and choice, when the trainee decides to learn, it is with an internal commitment that will help sustain the application of learning back on the job.

Here are some suggestions for facilitating participant learning:

◆ Warmly greet people as they arrive at the training room. Find out where they work, what they hope to get out of the session, and some of the challenges they face.

◆ Write key questions, quotes, and provocative statements related to the topic on flipchart pages and post them around the room.

- Create a comfortable aural environment by playing soothing music (classical or light jazz recommended) as people enter the training room.

- Establish the expectation of participant involvement early in the session. For example, you might begin a session by asking the large group a provocative question about the topic to immediately engage trainees in the content and encourage active participation.

- Have participants formally interact with each other within the first 20 to 30 minutes. This "ice-breaker" can be an exercise in goal setting, sharing key questions, or simply getting to know one another. The point of the ice-breaker is to create a safe and welcoming environment.

- Find a way to value every contribution, no matter how far off the subject or abstruse the trainee's comments or questions might be. People are taking a risk when they volunteer ideas or offer questions. Honor and respect what people offer by establishing a link between what they have said and the key point you are making.

- Establish ground rules for discussions and information sharing that help create confidentiality and safety. Encourage people to state their honest perceptions, experiences, and thoughts without fear that what they share during the session will be used against them.

- Establish the expectation early in the session that participants are responsible for their own learning. Indicate that you will provide a framework for learning and offer them useful information, tools, and tips, but that learning, if it occurs, is primarily their responsibility.

- Stay connected to the group. Read the signs of involvement or boredom and respond accordingly by sustaining the energy or dealing with the boredom by switching gears or changing direction.

- Use breaks to interact with participants. Find out if they are engaged, learning, frustrated, energized, or anxious. Talk to a variety of people to gather multiple perspectives.

- Use people's names.

- Refer to specific comments, ideas, questions, or suggestions offered by participants earlier in the session.

- When asked a content question by a participant, use the question as a teaching opportunity and turn the question back to the group to answer (and formulate your own response while the group responds).

- Vary the pace and methods of your instruction. Use different techniques throughout the session to engage participants in new ways.

There are many additional training design and facilitation tools, tips, and resources. Check the bibliography at the end of this book and join professional associations, such as the American Society for Training & Development (ASTD). ASTD and other human resource professional associations are a rich reservoir of knowledge and skills that will be an invaluable resource as you develop and deliver training programs.

What to Do Next

- Join the local chapter of ASTD or another human resources professional association, such as the Society for Human Resource Management.

- Begin planning your change leadership training sessions using the suggested session designs in the chapters that follow.

- Adjust and modify the suggested sessions based upon your objectives, audience, time available, and your own teaching style and preferences.

- Get approval and commitment for the proposed training program and its objectives from the leadership at all organizational levels.

- Practice. Consider the first session a "pilot" and debrief with a few participants to help you make adjustments to the training content and design.

- Facilitate the transfer of training by encouraging managers to support trainee participation prior to and following the session.

- Read the next chapter on evaluating learning outcomes.

◆ ◆ ◆

The next chapter explores ideas and strategies for evaluating the learning outcomes of your leading change workshops. The chapter will also enable you to make improvements to your training program design based upon participant reactions.

Evaluating Training Programs

- Assessing the four levels of learning and behavior change

- Assessing return-on-investment

As we've learned from our discussion of the transfer of learning from the workshop to the workplace, there's a lot more to training than designing and delivering a great program. Closely related to the issue of transfer is the matter of evaluating if learning has occurred and whether this learning has translated into concrete results for the organization.

In 1959, Donald Kirkpatrick published a four-part series titled "Techniques for Evaluating Training Programs" in the *Training Director's Journal*. This seminal article was followed in 1993 by the book *Evaluating Training Programs: The Four Levels,* which describes guidelines and suggested forms and procedures for each level. His four-level model continues to be the standard method for evaluating training programs. The four evaluation levels offered by Kirkpatrick—and an additional level—are highlighted in figure 5–1. Let's look at each in some detail and explore some strategies for measuring results for each of them.

Level 1: Participant Reaction and Intention

The first level of evaluation gathers data on both the participants' overall reaction to the training environment and their intentions beyond the training program itself. There are two possible opportunities for conducting a Level 1 evaluation: during the training and at its conclusion. Here are some ideas for assessing participants' reactions for each.

Figure 5–1

A Model for Training Evaluation

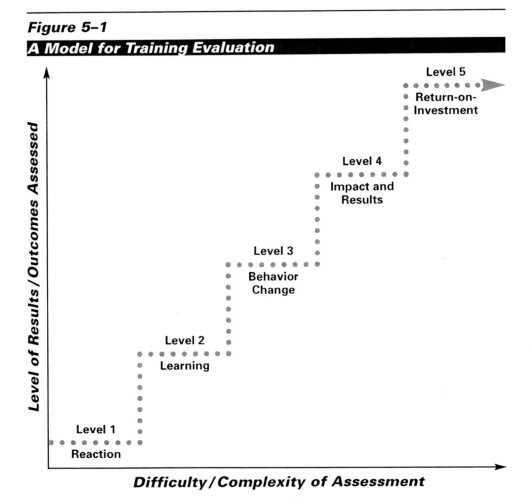

During the training:

◆ Conduct periodic "checks" of participants' reactions at key transition points. This might include taking time for a break to ask individual participants how the training is going by asking such questions as are we addressing the right things and is the pace too fast, too slow, or just right?

◆ Observe participants' body language, which may indicate satisfaction, engagement, boredom, or anxiety. Before taking action in response to these "readings," however, ensure that you check their accuracy with the group.

◆ Before taking a break near the midpoint of the session, ask participants to jot down on an index card one or two words that describe what they are feeling. Have them pass their cards to you. Review the cards at the break and, if possible, make needed adjustments for the balance of the program.

- Ask participants as a group to share their midcourse reactions and insights (are they learning the right things?)

At the end of the training, a Level 1 approach might include such things as

- Distributing a "smile sheet" at the last break before the session ends. Invite the attendees to complete the reaction forms before they leave.

- Asking selected participants to meet with you immediately after the program. In this debriefing, to which you have invited them several days earlier, ask them to share their thoughts on what worked, what didn't, and how the training could be improved.

- Distributing sticky notes to all participants. Invite them to write what they liked and suggestions for improving the program, one idea or comment per note. Divide a flipchart page into two columns: *What I liked about the session* and *Suggestions for improving the training*. Ask attendees to place their notes in the appropriate column as they leave the session.

- Guiding participants in action planning. Ask them what their intentions are for after the session. Have them share their plans with each other, with a few sharing their plans with the large group.

Level 2: Participant Learning

This evaluation level gathers data on whether the participants actually learned the core competencies that the program sought to teach. Level 2 goes beyond the reaction sheet by exploring what the participant actually learned from the training program. For example: Did the participants in a training program on performance coaching actually learn the core skills, knowledge, attitudes, and behaviors that we sought to develop?

Some approaches for Level 2 evaluation include

- quizzes that measure the learning of concepts and terms

- case applications that require the demonstration of knowledge or skill and allow the trainer to know that the participants are learning

- ◆ assessing the accuracy of responses to questions that ask participants to integrate the concepts taught

- ◆ role playing that enables trainees to demonstrate the learning and integration of key concepts, methods, and skills into behaviors

- ◆ guiding trainees' action planning to ensure that their plans reflect the course content

- ◆ conducting tests before and after training to measure the participants' acquisition of core content

- ◆ administering follow-up surveys to assess what learning trainees report following the training.

Level 3: Behavior Change

This level measures the degree to which the trainees were able to successfully apply what they learned back on their jobs. The learning to be assessed includes knowledge, skills, attitudes, and behaviors.

Level 3 goes beyond learning by exploring on-the-job performance. For example, participants may have learned how to reduce employees' resistance to change, but did they have success in actually reducing resistance to a specific change? Did they successfully use the skills and knowledge that they learned in the training program?

Here are some ideas for Level 3 learning assessment:

- ◆ Contact trainees and ask for reports of changes in themselves resulting from the training. Do they report changes in attitudes and behaviors?

- ◆ Conduct assessments of behavior change as perceived by others. Do the participants' supervisors, staffs, or peers report changes in targeted attitudes and behaviors?

- ◆ Make follow-up observations. From your own perspective, do participants demonstrate the new behaviors in their daily work?

Level 4: Impact and Results

The fourth level of evaluation measures the impact of the learned and applied training competencies on the organization's business. The key question explored with this level of evaluation is: Did the on-the-job application produce measurable results?

Level 4 evaluation is less interested in changed behavior itself than in whether the changed behavior led to tangible and positive outcomes for the business. For example, training participants provided the appropriate direction and support in the Exploration and Discovery phase of the change process, but has employee commitment to the change increased? Has employee anxiety decreased?

You may want to consider these approaches for Level 4 learning assessment:

- Gather data before and after training on aspects of organizational performance that could be affected positively by the training's content. This data might include such things as reductions in employee turnover, faster implementation of key steps in the change process, less overtime, higher customer satisfaction, increased sales, or greater employee commitment to performance improvement.

- Conduct surveys of customers, supervisors, staff, peers, and other stakeholders to determine whether these groups perceive improvement in key organizational outcomes.

- Compare the performance of those who received the training with the performance of those who did not receive the training.

Level 5: Return-on-Investment

Kirkpatrick's four levels of assessment have served the training world well over the years. Kirkpatrick suggests that organizations begin evaluation by using Level 1 for all programs (which he describes as customer satisfaction) and continue through Levels 2, 3, and 4. Organizations that begin evaluation at Level 3 or 4 are making a mistake, Kirkpatrick suggests.

In recent years, however, there has been a growing interest in moving beyond business outcomes to explore whether, on balance, the training generated a financial benefit for the organization that, ideally, more than offset the costs of the program. Thus the emergence of a new Level 5 or return-on-investment (ROI) assessment.

Level 5 evaluation measures the actual financial benefits experienced by the business that directly resulted from the applied training competencies. The key question explored with this level of evaluation is: Did the monetary value of the results exceed the cost for designing and conducting the training program?

Level 5 evaluation quantifies the tangible, positive outcomes for the business in financial terms and then compares this return with the total investment in the training. For example: Employee turnover has been reduced by 30 percent since the company implemented a training program in change leadership. How does this reduction translate into actual dollars saved by the company and what was the overall cost of the training program itself?

The costs associated with delivering a program can be extensive. Costs that should be included in an ROI calculation are time for needs assessment, program development, materials development, participants' time away from their jobs, duplication of materials, evaluation costs, and follow-up strategies to reinforce learning.

Level 5 assessments are far less common than all the other levels. If you're interested in exploring this assessment realm, we encourage you to read some of the resources listed in the Further Reading section. Perhaps the most useful reference is Jack Phillips' book, *Return on Investment in Training and Performance Improvement Programs: A Step-By-Step Manual for Calculating the Financial Return on Investment* (1997).

What to Do Next

- Design an approach that considers all four levels.

- Take steps to include all four levels in your evaluation plan.

- Review Training Tool 10–4, Chapter 10, page 189, for possible assessment issues to include when developing your customized workshop evaluation form and process.

- Read the recommended books on determining ROI for the change leadership program.

◆ ◆ ◆

The next chapter is the first of three that present sample workshop agendas. You'll first explore the content of a briefing for executives on leading change.

Two-Hour Executive Briefing on Change

- Objectives, materials, and step-by-step preparations for the Executive Briefing on Change
- Sample program agenda
- Executive Briefing training instrument and handout
- Executive Briefing PowerPoint slides

The first requirement for successfully leading organization-wide change is helping executives gain insight on the change process and how to lead people through change. Without this key knowledge on the part of an organization's leaders, its change efforts are more likely to fail.

This chapter presents a two-hour program—called the Executive Briefing on Change—that can be used as an initial strategy for developing critical knowledge and awareness in key executives. Because not all organizational change is directed from the executive office, however, this briefing can also be used to educate any group that is defining needed changes and seeking to drive them through an organization or one of its units.

Training Objectives

The objectives of the Executive Briefing on Change are to

- identify the reasons for initiating an organizational change
- recognize the impact that change has on the organization, employees, customers, and other stakeholders

- understand the importance of a clear vision for change or for desired results

- develop a thoughtful strategy for effectively implementing change and sustaining employee commitment to the change.

Materials

For the instructor:

- Learning Activity 9–1: Perceptions of Change

- Learning Activity 9–2: Experiencing Personal Change

- Learning Activity 9–3: Guiding People through the Change Journey

- Flipchart and marking pens

- PowerPoint slides 6–1 through 6–18. To access slides for this program, open the file *Executive Briefing.ppt* on the accompanying CD. Reference copies of the slides for this training session are included at the end of this chapter.

For the participants:

- Training Instrument 6–1: Characteristics of and Actions for Each Phase in the Change Journey

- Handout 6–1: Components of a Change Implementation Plan

- Handout 9–1: The Journey through Change

- Handout 9–2: Suggested Actions for Helping People through Change

- Handout 9–3: An Integrated Model for Leading Change

- Handout 9–4: Actions for Introducing and Leading Change

- Handout 9–7: Common Forces Causing Change

Preparations

Before the Executive Briefing on Change session:

1. Meet with a representative or representatives from the executive leadership group to discuss the change initiative and the importance of the Executive Briefing on Change to its success.

2. Schedule the session and secure a conference room far in advance to ensure that all key executives involved with the change are able to participate.

3. Design the program around the specific change initiative proposed by the executive group (or the group that is initiating the change) and your discussions during the advance meeting.

4. Prepare training materials (handouts, training instruments, instructions, PowerPoint presentation, and supporting audiovisual items).

5. Send a memo, letter, or email of invitation reiterating the purpose of the Executive Briefing on Change and its importance to the success of the change initiative.

6. Order food and beverages as necessary.

Just before the Executive Briefing on Change session:

1. Arrive early at the training room.

2. Verify room setup.

3. Set up and test such equipment as flipchart, markers, LCD projector, or overhead projector.

4. Prepare two flipchart pages titled "The Key Forces Causing Change" and "Next Steps for Change Implementation."

5. Place materials on tables.

6. Display PowerPoint 6–1 as a "Welcome" greeting to participants as they enter the training room.

Two-Hour Sample Agenda: Executive Briefing on Change

9:00 a.m.   Welcome (5 minutes)

Welcome participants to the Executive Briefing on Change session, display PowerPoint slide 6–2 as you highlight the objectives for the briefing and emphasize its importance as a key step in implementing the organization's change initiative.

9:05

Learning Activity 9–1: Perceptions of Change (chapter 9, pg. 119) (10 minutes)

Display PowerPoint slide 6–3 and facilitate this activity, which engages briefing participants in thinking about the impact of change on themselves and others.

9:15

Exploring the Journey through Change (25 minutes)

Distribute Handout 9–1 from Learning Activity 9–2: Experiencing Personal Change (chapter 9, page 123).

Display PowerPoint slide 6–4, introducing the Journey through Change model. Highlight the overall model and (borrowing from Learning Activity 9–2, step 17, page xx) offer a description of the natural and inevitable journey that all people experience as they move through a change.

Note the two dimensions of the model: (1) looking back versus looking forward and (2) stability versus chaos. Suggest that stable environments create conditions that support Comfort and Control, and that being comfortable and in control involves holding on to what we have (looking back). Indicate that as change is introduced, the stable environment begins to descend into instability or even chaos. The fear, anger, and resistance people often feel as stability gradually disappears result from the loss of the comfort and control that they experienced in the past.

Suggest that people who don't flee back to Comfort and Control (and a state of denial) at the greatest point of instability and chaos, or who don't fight the change, begin to abandon the past and, with varying degrees of enthusiasm, begin making efforts to create a new stability and make the change work for them (looking forward).

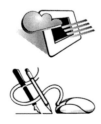

Display PowerPoint slides 6–5 through 6–8, noting the characteristics usually experienced by those affected by a change in each phase of the process. Distribute Training Instrument 6–1.

Display PowerPoint slide 6–9, the Journey through Change (same as slide 6–4). Highlight some of the characteristics of the model (as cited in step 17 of Learning Activity 9–2, page 123).

9:40   Leader Actions for Guiding People through Change—a variation on Learning Activity 9–3: Guiding People through the Change Journey (page 134) (35 minutes)

Guide participants through the first four steps of Learning Activity 9–3. Refer to Training Instrument 6–1 (page 59). Ask participants to work individually as they identify at least two actions that they can each take as leaders to guide people through each phase of change and into the next phase (or, for Learning, Acceptance, and Commitment, actions they can take to sustain progress and avoid the drift back into Comfort and Control). Give participants approximately five minutes for this individual activity.

After about five minutes, reconvene the group and ask participants to offer their suggestions for key actions that leaders can take at each phase.

Display PowerPoint slides 6–10 through 6–13, highlighting the recommended actions for change leaders and reinforcing the actions that were offered by participants. Distribute Handout 9–2, which summarizes these suggested actions.

Display PowerPoint slide 6–14 and distribute Handouts 9–3 and 9–4 (An Integrated Model for Leading Change and Actions for Introducing and Leading Change). Note that Handout 9–3 is an integrated model for introducing a change and that Handout 9–4 identifies the actions that leaders should take to introduce the change while responding to the emotional journey people tend to take during the change process.

Ask participants to take a few minutes to read and reflect on the actions noted in both Handouts 9–2 and 9–4.

Suggest that the actions leaders take in introducing a change actually precipitate the emotional response of those affected by it and that leaders must not only nudge people into the next phase of the change journey but also respond to the emotional needs people have in the current phase.

Note the overlap of actions suggested in Handout 9–4 with those in Training Instrument 9–4, suggesting that many of the same actions that leaders will take in introducing a change involve responding to where people are on their own emotional journeys during the change process.

10:15   Taking the First Step: Creating a Felt Need (15 minutes)

Emphasize the importance of the first step of introducing a change (creating a felt need), as shown in Handout 9–2. Suggest that leaders tend not to spend enough time making the case as to why a change is needed.

Note that if people who are affected by the coming change don't know the reasons behind it or if they don't see the reasons for themselves, they will be less likely to move out of "Comfort and Control."

Display PowerPoint slide 6–15 and distribute Training Instrument 9–7. Briefly discuss the common external and internal forces for change. Invite participants to pair up and discuss what they view as the key forces driving change in the organization and the consequences of *not* responding to these forces.

After two to three minutes, reconvene the group and draw out comments. Record responses on the prepared flipchart page. Remind participants that these drivers of change (and the consequences of not responding to them) are the reasons behind the change that leaders must "amplify" to help create the felt need for change.

Suggest that sufficient attention must be paid to creating this felt need for change or people will simply ignore the new ideas, thinking, "this too shall pass."

Stress that once the change is introduced and people begin to feel the need for it, the leader must continue to understand where people are in their emotional journeys during the change process. The leader must respond in appropriate and timely fashion, with the actions and strategies that have been discussed and were summarized on Handouts 9–2 and 9–4.

10:30   Identifying Components of a Change Implementation Plan (20 minutes)

Suggest that the next action for the executive group is to develop some preliminary "next steps" for introducing the change and preparing for the reactions of those affected. Display PowerPoint slide 6–16 and distribute Handout 6–1 (on page 61).

Note that in order to create a successful change initiative, the leadership group must develop a plan for implementing change that integrates the issues that have been discussed during this briefing (and some that haven't been discussed). Indicate that the actions that should be included in this plan are

- creating a change leadership "design team"

- documenting the case for change—identifying the forces causing the change and the impact of these forces on the organization's future success

- developing the change "vision" or desired result

- defining the impacts on those affected by the change —the likely perceived losses and hidden opportunities from the change

- developing a formal implementation strategy

- identifying measures of success (how the success of the planned change will be evaluated)

- developing a communication strategy

- developing a training strategy for leaders, managers, supervisors, employees, and (if appropriate) customers, suppliers, and other key stakeholders.

10:50   Identifying Next Steps for Change Implementation (10 minutes)

Facilitate a discussion that identifies the next steps for moving ahead and developing a change implementation plan. Encourage the group to identify an individual or group who will be responsible for leading the development of the change implementation plan (this may be the change leadership "design team").

End the session with an agreement by the executive group on a tentative implementation timeline.

11:00   Close

Display PowerPoint slide 6–17, noting the importance of creating a change plan that enables people to feel that "we did it all by ourselves."

Display PowerPoint slide 6–18 and thank participants for taking part in the Executive Briefing on Change.

What to Do Next

- Become a member of or work closely with the change leadership design team to integrate change training workshops for managers, supervisors, staff, and other stakeholders into the change implementation strategy.

- Develop a change training plan in support of the change implementation plan.

- Design and develop training programs for managers, supervisors, and staff.

- Identify other stakeholder groups that may require the change training and design customized workshops for these groups, based upon the training agendas and learning activities included within this book.

◆ ◆ ◆

The next chapter includes an agenda and supporting learning activities for a change training workshop for managers and supervisors.

Training Instrument 6–1
Characteristics of and Leader Actions for Each Phase in the Change Journey

Characteristics of Each Phase of the Change Journey

As people experience change they travel an emotional journey that moves them from "comfort and control" through "anger, fear, and resistance" and "exploration and discovery" into "learning and commitment."

The emotional responses you are likely to observe in others as they respond to each phase of the journey through change are listed below in the left-hand column.

Leader Actions to Guide People through the Change Journey

What do people need from change leaders as they try to move people from "comfort and control" toward "learning and commitment"?

Identify specific actions that change leaders should take to deal with the issues, concerns, and emotional needs of people at each phase. For "learning and commitment," identify actions that reinforce the change and sustain continuous learning and improvement.

PHASE OF THE JOURNEY THROUGH CHANGE	ACTIONS OF THE CHANGE LEADER
Comfort and control Comfortable Safe Everything's fine Happy Satisfied No problems Positive Rewarding I'm okay, you're okay!	
Fear, anger, and resistance Frustration Anger Fearful Betrayed Upset Confused Hostility Anxiety Self-Doubt Lost Dazed Challenged	

continued on next page

Training Instrument 6–1, continued
Characteristics of and Leader Actions for Each Phase in the Change Journey

PHASE OF THE JOURNEY THROUGH CHANGE	ACTIONS OF THE CHANGE LEADER
Inquiry, experimentation, and discovery Confused Questioning Hopeful Opportunity Frustrated Disappointed. Challenged Half-way there! Making progress Going in all directions at once! Searching for solutions Exciting Innovation/creativity	
Learning, acceptance, and commitment Now I know Energized Success! We made it! Relief Wow! Self-confidence Satisfied Comfortable What's next?	

Handout 6-1
Components of a Change Implementation Plan

These are the core elements of any successful plan for implementing organizational change. Some of the key questions that the change implementation plan should address are identified.

- **Create a leading change design team**—Who must be involved in helping you move your organization or work area in a new direction? What areas, teams, or individuals should be involved in designing the change?

- **Document the case for change**—What are the forces causing the change and what is the impact of these forces on the organization's future success? Why is there a need for change? What departments, units, teams, or individuals are affected and to what degree? Do the forces causing change suggest a modest, incremental, or transformational change? What are the consequences to the organization of not responding effectively to these forces?

- **Develop a preliminary vision for the change**—What is the change that needs to occur? What do we need to accomplish or achieve as a result of the change? What problem are we trying to solve? What will the outcomes of the change look like?

- **Define the effects on those affected by the change**—What are the potential pros and cons of the change for the organization, departments, units, teams, and individuals? Who benefits and who loses? Are customers or other stakeholders affected and to what extent?

- **Create your preliminary strategy and action plan**—How will you raise awareness of the need for change? How will the losses be reduced, eliminated, or managed? How will employees and other stakeholders be involved in developing the change vision and strategy? What actions will build commitment to the change? How will the benefits from the change be realized? What actions need to occur, when should they occur, and who should take the lead in taking them? What is the implementation timeline?

- **Identify measures of success**—How will the success of the planned change be evaluated? What are the key indicators or measures of success? What benchmarks along the way will be used to help track the progress the organization is making?

- **Develop your communication strategy**—Who needs to be kept informed of the change vision and strategy? What are the methods for communicating with these key stakeholders? What is the ideal frequency of the communications about the change and the progress being made?

- **Develop your training strategy**—What is your plan for building change leadership skills and knowledge in leaders, managers, supervisors, employees, and (if appropriate) customers, suppliers, and other key stakeholders? What is your timeline for training in relation to the change implementation strategy?

Slide 6–1

Welcome to . . .

Executive Briefing on Change

An Overview of the Impact of Change and How to Introduce Organizational Change

Slide 6–2

Today's Agenda . . .

- Identify the reasons for initiating a change.
- Recognize the impact that change has on the organization, employees, customers, and other stakeholders.
- Understand the importance of a clear change vision.
- Develop a thoughtful strategy for effective change implementation and sustaining employee commitment to the change.

Slide 6–3

Your Perceptions of Change

What are your reactions when you hear the word "change"?

- Negative perceptions
- Positive perceptions

Slide 6–4

The Journey Through Change

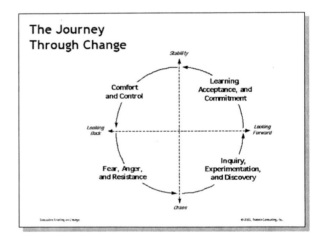

Slide 6–5

Characteristics of *Comfort and Control*

- Comfortable
- Safe
- Everything's fine
- Happy
- Satisfied
- No problems
- Positive
- Rewarding
- In control . . .
- I'm okay, you're okay!

People feel comfortable, safe, and in control. They are working hard — but often on the wrong things.

Slide 6–6

Characteristics of *Fear, Anger, and Resistance*

- Frustration
- Anger
- Fearful
- Betrayed
- Upset
- Confused
- Challenged
- Hostility
- Anxiety
- Self-doubt
- Lost
- Dazed

People feel frustrated, angry, and fearful about the change. Performance deteriorates.

Slide 6–7

Characteristics of *Inquiry, Experimentation, and Discovery*

- Confused
- Questioning
- Hopeful
- Opportunity
- Frustrated
- Disappointed
- Challenged
- Half-way there!
- Making progress

- Going in all directions at once!
- Searching for solutions
- Exciting!
- Innovation/creativity

People want to make the change work — on their terms as well as those of the organization — but they don't have clear answers.

Slide 6–8

Characteristics of *Learning, Acceptance, and Commitment*

- Now I know!
- Energized
- Success!
- We made it!
- Relief
- Wow!
- Self-confidence
- Satisfied
- Comfortable
- What's next?

People are focused on and excited about the future. They begin working together to accomplish the change vision.

Slide 6–9

The Journey Through Change

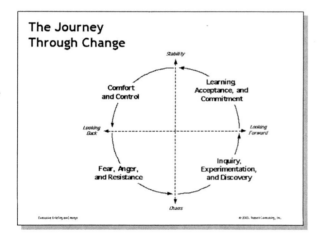

Slide 6–10

Actions for *Comfort and Control*

- Acknowledge their successful past.
- Get people's attention!
- Sell the need for change . . . sell the pain and the consequences of *not* changing.
- Immerse people in information about the change . . . customer complaints, budget data, increasing costs, competitive pressures.
- Let people know it will happen— one way or another!
- Give people time to let the ideas sink in.
- Don't sell the solutions . . . sell the problem!

Slide 6–11

Actions for *Fear, Anger, and Resistance*

- Co-create the vision.
- Listen, listen, listen.
- Acknowledge people's pain, perceived losses, and anger.
- Strive to address their perceived losses.
- Tell people what you know— and what you *don't* know.
- Don't try to talk people out of their feelings.
- Discuss ways to *solve* the problems people see with the change.
- Encourage discussion, dissent, disagreement, debate . . . keep people talking.

Slide 6–12

Actions for *Inquiry, Experimentation, and Discovery*

- Give people freedom and direction.
- Give people permission to find their own solutions.
- Encourage people to take risks.
- Refine the vision — make room for others' ideas.
- Tell people as much as you know.
- Encourage teamwork and collaboration.
- Encourage personal reflection and learning.
- Provide people training and support.
- Set short-term goals.

Slide 6–13

Actions for _Learning, Acceptance, and Commitment_

- Acknowledge their hard work.
- Celebrate successes and accomplishments.
- Reaffirm the vision.
- Bring people together toward the vision.
- Acknowledge what people have left behind.
- Develop long-term goals and plans.
- Provide tools and training to reinforce new behaviors.
- Reinforce and reward the new behaviors.
- Create systems and structures that reinforce new behaviors.
- Prepare people for the next change.

Slide 6–14

The Integrated Change Leadership Model . . .

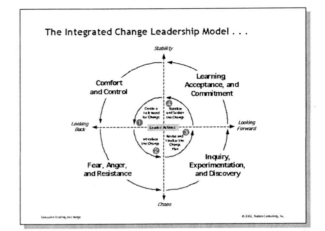

Slide 6–15

The Forces for Change . . .

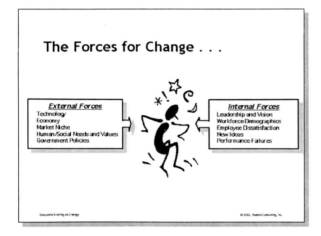

Slide 6–16

Components of a Change Plan

- Create a leading change design team.
- Document the case for change.
- Develop a preliminary vision for the change.
- Define the impacts on those affected by the change.
- Create your preliminary strategy and action plan.
- Identify measures of success.
- Develop your communication strategy.
- Develop your training strategy.

Slide 6–17

The master doesn't talk, he acts. When his work is done, the people say "Amazing! We did it all by ourselves."

— Lao-Tzu
Author of _Tao Te Ching_
500 BC

Slide 6–18

Thank You!!

- Don't forget the emotional impact change has on people.

- Develop a thoughtful change implementation plan and strategy.

Workshops for Managers and Supervisors

What's in This Chapter?

- Objectives, materials, and step-by-step preparations for the one-day Leading Change Workshop for Managers and Supervisors

- Objectives, materials, and step-by-step preparations for the half-day Follow-Up Workshop for Managers and Supervisors

- Sample one-day and half-day workshop agendas

- PowerPoint slides for the workshops

Successful change initiatives depend upon managers and supervisors taking an active role in introducing the change and then guiding people through the emotional journey that change often causes. Without effective leadership from those to whom they look for guidance, direction, support, and feedback, employees of an organization going through change are likely to be perplexed, confused, angry, frustrated, and openly resistant to new ways of doing business. That's why this workshop for managers and supervisors is so important. Without strong managerial and supervisory leadership, employee commitment to the change will take longer to achieve or may fail to take hold at all.

This chapter presents a one-day workshop designed to help managers and supervisors develop critical knowledge and skills concerning their responsibilities for leading change for their departments, teams, or organizational units. An additional half-day follow-up workshop is offered as an option to help integrate, reinforce, and enhance participant learning approximately six to nine weeks after the original one-day workshop.

One-Day Leading Change Workshop for Managers and Supervisors

TRAINING OBJECTIVES

The objectives of the workshop are to

- recognize the impact that change has on employees and how it might affect customers and other stakeholders

- identify the actions that leaders and staff can take to enable the most healthy response to change

- describe the forces behind organizational change and the implications for the organization

- develop resilience in those affected by the change

- develop a plan for guiding people through the change.

MATERIALS

For the instructor:

- Learning Activity 9–1: Perceptions of Change

- Learning Activity 9–2: Experiencing Personal Change

- Learning Activity 9–3: Guiding People through the Change Journey

- Learning Activity 9–4: Introducing and Leading a Change

- Learning Activity 9–5: The Forces Causing Change

- Learning Activity 9–6: The Sources of Change Resistance

- Learning Activity 9–7: Identifying the Perceived Losses and Exploring the Opportunities from a Proposed Change

- Learning Activity 9–8: Strengthening Change Resilience

- Tool 10–1: Training Room Configuration

- Tool 10–2: Ah Ha! Sheet

- Tool 10–3: Goal-Setting Worksheet

- Tool 10–4: Topics to Include in the Training Evaluation Form

- Flipchart and marking pens

◆ PowerPoint slides 7–1 through 7–42. To access slides for this program, open the file *Leading Change–Managers.ppt* on the accompanying CD. Copies of the slides for this training session are included at the end of this chapter.

For the participants:

◆ Training Instrument 9–1: Perceptions of Change

◆ Training Instrument 9–2: Experiencing Personal Change

◆ Training Instrument 9–3: Characteristics of and Actions for Each Phase of the Change Journey

◆ Training Instrument 9–4: Personal Plan for Helping Yourself and Others through Change

◆ Training Instrument 9–5: Introducing, Leading, and Sustaining Commitment to a Change

◆ Training Instrument 9–6: Personal Plan for Initiating and Sustaining a Change

◆ Training Instrument 9–7: Common Forces Causing Change

◆ Training Instrument 9–8: Responding to the Forces for Change

◆ Training Instrument 9–9: The Origins of Change Resistance

◆ Training Instrument 9–10: Personal Plan for Dealing with Change Resistance

◆ Training Instrument 9–11: The Perceived Losses of Change

◆ Training Instrument 9–12: Personal Plan for Action—Dealing with the Perceived Losses

◆ Training Instrument 9–13: Characteristics of Change Resilience

◆ Training Instrument 9–14: Personal Plan for Strengthening Resilience in Others

◆ Handout 9–1: The Journey through Change

◆ Handout 9–2: Suggested Action to Help People through Change

◆ Handout 9–3: An Integrated Model for Leading Change

◆ Handout 9–4: Actions for Introducing and Leading Change

- Handout 9–5: Why We Value Change Resisters

- Handout 9–6: The Crisis of Change

- Handout 9–6: Human Nature and the Character of Change

- Tool 10–2: Ah Ha! Sheet

- Tool 10–3: Goal-Setting Worksheet

PREPARATIONS

Before the workshop:

1. If appropriate, meet with a representative or representatives from the attendee group to discuss their expectations for the Leading Change Workshop.

2. Schedule the session and secure a training room for the one-day workshop. If the half-day follow-up workshop detailed in this chapter is planned, schedule this session and room at the same time.

3. Design the program around the proposed change initiative and make sure that it reflects the priorities of the executive group (or the group that is initiating the change).

4. Prepare training materials (handouts, training instruments, instructions, tools, training program evaluation form, PowerPoint presentation, and supporting audiovisual materials).

5. Send a memo, letter, or email of invitation to participants reiterating the purpose of the Leading Change Workshop and its importance in identifying and developing their roles in the success of the change initiative.

6. Order food and beverages as necessary.

Just prior to the workshop:

1. Arrive early at the training room.

2. Verify room setup.

3. Set up and test such equipment as flipchart, markers, LCD projector, or overhead projector.

4. Prepare and post flipchart pages titled "Your Goals/Questions" and "Parking Lot," and additional flipchart pages as detailed in the Learning Activities. You may also want to post another flipchart page highlighting key questions to be addressed during the workshop (that relate to the objectives).

5. Place materials on tables.

6. Display PowerPoint slide 7–1 as a welcome and greeting to partici- pants as they enter the training room.

7. Greet participants individually as they enter the training room.

ONE-DAY SAMPLE AGENDA: LEADING CHANGE WORKSHOP FOR MANAGERS AND SUPERVISORS

8:30 a.m.   Welcome (5 minutes)

Welcome participants to the Leading Change Workshop for Managers and Supervisors, introduce yourself, highlight the main purpose of the workshop, and emphasize the importance of the session as a key step in implementing change in their organization.

8:35   Learning Activity 9–1: Perceptions of Change (chapter 9,  page 119) (10 minutes)

This activity quickly gets participants to begin reflecting on their positive and negative perceptions of change and begins the dialogue about why people may resist change initiatives.

8:45   Goal Setting (30 minutes)

Make the transition from the preceding activity by linking the exploration of why people's perceptions might end up in the "negative" column and the importance of using the time in the workshop to find ways to help create positive outcomes from change initiatives.

Review the specific goals and roadmap for the workshop with PowerPoint slides 7–3 and 7–4.

Distribute the Goal-Setting Worksheet (Tool 10–3, chapter 10, page 187). Ask participants to identify

- their personal objectives for the workshop and how likely it is that they will realize these objectives through this training session

- what's in it for them if they achieve their objective and how likely it is that this "reward" will occur

- how important this positive benefit or reward is to them. (*Note:* This three-step process of goal setting is based upon the Expectancy Theory of motivation [see books by Vroom and by Porter and Lawler, listed in the Further Reading section].)

After a couple of minutes, display PowerPoint slide 7–5 and ask participants to work in their small groups to (a) meet and greet; (b) share their personal objectives (the first of the questions on the Goal-Setting Worksheet); and (c) identify, as a group, two or three questions about leading change that the group would like to address during the workshop. Give the small groups approximately seven minutes for this activity.

Have the groups report their questions and record these on the prepared flipchart page. Highlight the importance of the attendees taking responsibility for their own learning by seeking out the answers to these questions as they work their way through the workshop.

Indicate that you have posted a "Parking Lot" (the flipchart page) as a place to record additional concerns and questions that you may not be able to address today. Encourage them to identify these "parking lot" concerns that can be "parked" at any time to ensure that it is retained for future consideration.

Distribute the Ah Ha! Sheet (Tool 10–2, chapter 10, page 185). Emphasize the importance of the attendees making notes on this Ah Ha! Sheet throughout day, based upon what they hear, see, and learn. Encourage them to be active participants in their own learning by using the Ah Ha!

Sheet to record the key learning moments and insights that will be most useful to them beyond today's session.

Note the schedule for breaks and lunch, and the location of restrooms, telephones, and refreshments.

9:15 Learning Activity 9–2: Experiencing Personal Change (chapter 9, page 123) (50 minutes)

Guide participants through this activity to help them see the pattern in their emotional response to change.

10:05 Break (15 minutes)

10:20 Learning Activity 9–3: Guiding People through the Change Journey (chapter 9, page 134) (50 minutes)

This activity helps participants understand how they can ease their own journeys through change, as well as those of others.

11:10 Learning Activity 9–4: Introducing and Leading a Change (chapter 9, page 140) (50 minutes)

Building upon the actions that leaders can take to help people along the emotional journey of change, this learning activity introduces a four-phased model for introducing and sustaining change.

Noon Lunch (60 minutes)

1:00 p.m. Learning Activity 9–5: The Forces Causing Change (chapter 9, page 148) (45 minutes)

This activity asks participants to examine the forces that tend to cause change in general and the specific situation their organization is facing that is the underlying cause of the needed change.

1:45 Learning Activity 9–6: The Sources of Change Resistance (chapter 9, page 154) (35 minutes)

This is a transitional activity that moves participants from examining the forces for change (the key change drivers) to the discussion of the source of resistance. Although the morning discussion identified resistance as one aspect of the four phases of the emotional journey, this activity delves deeper into why people might work against a change.

2:20 Break (15 minutes)

2:35 Learning Activity 9–7: Identifying the Perceived Losses and Exploring the Opportunities from a Proposed Change (chapter 9, page 161) (45 minutes)

Continuing the discussion of one key source of change resistance, this activity guides participants in anticipating the losses that those affected by the change may perceive and the "hidden" opportunities that change provides to those who are open to them.

3:20 Learning Activity 9–8: Strengthening Change Resilience (chapter 9, page 169) (45 minutes)

The final learning activity of the Leading Change Workshop for Managers and Supervisors introduces the concept of resilience—the human capacity to spring back in the face of adversity. The activity also guides participants in developing strategies for strengthening resilience in those most affected by the proposed change.

4:05 Integration and Conclusion (20 minutes)

Tie together the various elements of the workshop content and review the questions the group identified earlier in the day in the goal-setting segment. Ask participants to bring up questions that have not yet been addressed during the workshop. Depending upon time available, you can either assign these questions to the small groups or facilitate a group discussion of them.

In conclusion, emphasize that leading change (as noted by Machiavelli in the quote shared earlier) is often a thankless job, but that each of them has the opportunity—actually the responsibility—to make the process work for both those who are affected by the change and for their organization.

Encourage them to take the next step and integrate the various elements of their action plans that they developed throughout the day into their daily work.

If the half-day follow-up "check-in" workshop is planned, remind them of the date of the session and of their assignment for that follow-up session.

4:25   Evaluation (5 minutes)

Display PowerPoint slide 7–42. Thank the participants for attending the Leading Change Workshop and for their active involvement throughout the session. Distribute the training program evaluation form and encourage participants to leave the completed forms at their tables or at a designated location.

4:30   Close

Half-Day Follow-Up Leading Change Workshop for Managers and Supervisors

TRAINING OBJECTIVES

The objectives of the half-day Follow-Up Workshop on Leading Change are to

- review the integrated model for leading change

- answer questions about the integrated model

- discuss the progress the participants are making in helping people through organizational change

- identify additional steps participants can take to enhance their change leadership abilities.

MATERIALS

For the instructor:

- Flipchart and marking pens

- PowerPoint slides 7–43 through 7–49. To access slides for this program, open the file *Follow-Up (Managers).ppt* on the accompanying

CD. Reference copies of the slides for this training session are included at the end of this chapter.

For the participants:

- Training Instrument 7–1: Reflections on Leading Change
- Training Instrument 7–2: Next Steps for Leading Change

PREPARATIONS

Before the workshop:

1. Schedule the session and secure a training room prior to offering the initial one-day workshop for managers.

2. Prepare training materials (handouts, training instruments, instructions, tools, training program evaluation form, PowerPoint presentation, and supporting audiovisual materials).

3. Send a memo, letter, or email to participants in the full-day Leading Change Workshop reminding them of the half-day follow-up session and reiterating what they should be working on and be prepared to discuss/share at the follow-up session. Ask participants to bring copies of their handouts, tools, and training instruments from the full-day session.

4. Order food and beverages as necessary.

Just prior to the workshop:

1. Arrive early at the training room.

2. Verify room setup.

3. Set up and test such equipment as flipchart, markers, LCD projector, or overhead projector. You may wish to provide a flipchart easel with paper for each of the small-group tables. These flipcharts may be used by the groups in reporting their answers to questions assigned to them during the session.

4. Prepare and post flipchart two pages titled "Your Goals/Questions" and "Parking Lot."

5. Place materials on tables.

6. Display PowerPoint 7–43 as a "Welcome Back" greeting to participants as they enter the training room.

7. Greet participants individually as they enter the training room.

SAMPLE AGENDA: HALF-DAY FOLLOW-UP LEADING CHANGE WORKSHOP FOR MANAGERS AND SUPERVISORS

8:30 a.m.   Welcome (5 minutes)

Welcome returning participants to the follow-up session to the Leading Change Workshop for Managers and Supervisors. Display PowerPoint slide 7–44 while you highlight the main purpose of the follow-up workshop and emphasize the importance of this session as a "check" on the progress they have made with their staffs. Note that the Parking Lot (from the one-day session) is available and can be added to as new issues and questions emerge during this session.

8:35   Reflections on Leading Change (35 minutes)

Distribute Training Instrument 7–1 (page 80) and ask participants to work by themselves to reflect upon their change leadership efforts since the full-day workshop as they answer the questions on the handout. Give participants three to four minutes for this.

Reconvene the large group. Display PowerPoint slide 7–45 and ask people to meet in their small groups to (a) select a group leader; (b) meet and greet; (c) discuss what worked and what didn't work with their efforts to lead change; (d) discuss what remains unclear or confusing about their responsibilities and roles for leading change; and (e) develop two or three questions their group would like to have answered about leading change, their roles within it, and the models they explored at the day-long workshop. Give the small groups 8 to 10 minutes for this.

Facilitate a large-group discussion about what worked in their efforts to lead change and what didn't. Guide the groups in identifying questions on which they would like to focus during this workshop. Record the questions on the prepared flipchart page.

Indicate that after a brief review of the integrated model for leading change, much of the remaining time in the workshop will focus on exploring answers to their questions.

Facilitator Note: After group members offer their questions, you may want to identify which questions are best answered by you, by the participants themselves, or by parties not present, such as the executive change leadership group (change design team). You can invite the group to help you sort these questions by who might be in the best position to provide useful answers.

After you have personally reflected upon the questions (or asked the group to help you do this), point out that some of them may be best answered by people not present at the workshop and suggest that these questions can be added to the Parking Lot for future consideration and response by the appropriate party.

9:10   Review of Integrated Leading Change Model
(15 minutes)

Display PowerPoint slide 7–46, showing the integrated leading change model. Highlight the four phases of introducing or leading change (the inner circle) and then the four phases of the emotional journey that people make through change.

Note the actions that change leaders take to initiate a change and the additional actions they need to take to help people move through their emotional responses to change.

Respond to any questions identified by the small groups that directly relate to the integrated leading change model.

Refer to the appropriate materials from the full-day session as necessary.

9:25   Exploring Questions and Issues about Leading Change
        (90 minutes)

        Select the questions about leading change that seem
        most appropriate for the groups to answer themselves.
        Assign one or two questions to each of the small groups,
        taking care not to ask a group to answer its own ques-
        tion. You may want to assign some questions to more
        than one group, or, if a question seems critically impor-
        tant, assign it to all of the groups. (*Note:* You might find
        it useful and provocative to assign to the groups some of
        the change-specific questions that either you or the
        group earlier decided were best answered by people not
        present.)

        Display PowerPoint slide 7–47. Ask the groups to select a
        group leader and give the groups 10 to 15 minutes to de-
        velop answers to their assigned questions. If desired, you
        can direct the groups to write their recommended an-
        swers on flipchart paper that you have made available.

        While the small groups are developing their answers, de-
        velop possible responses to the questions that you can
        best answer.

        As time permits, check on each group's progress and pro-
        vide clarification and direction as necessary.

        Once the groups have developed responses to their as-
        signed questions, facilitate the process of them reporting
        their suggested answers.

        Take a break at an appropriate opportunity between group
        responses.

10:00   Break (15 minutes)

10:15   Exploring Questions and Issues about Leading Change
        (continued)

        Continue leading the group reporting process. Complete
        this segment of the workshop by providing your answers
        to key questions asked by the group. Organize and display
        appropriate PowerPoint slides from the full-day workshop

to assist you if required. For specific questions about the change itself that you are not able to answer, highlight the process for dealing with these Parking Lot questions with those not attending the session.

11:10   Next Steps for Leading Change (30 minutes)

Distribute Training Instrument 7–2 (page 81). Ask participants to reflect on the earlier "what worked/what didn't" discussion and the questions explored by the group as they identify their personal next steps for strengthening their change leadership. Give participants five to eight minutes for this.

After about five to eight minutes, ask participants to pair up and share their plans with their partners. Encourage them to help each other further refine and strengthen their plans for leading change. Give the pairs seven to eight minutes for sharing and refining their personal plans.

11:40   Integration (15 minutes)

Reconvene the group. Encourage them to continue strengthening their abilities to lead change. Recommend that they continue sharing what's working and what's not with others who have attended the workshop. Advise them to revisit and review their plans frequently as they continue to demonstrate their leadership in their decisions and actions with others.

Indicate that you will be sending them a reminder (via memo or email) in four to six weeks to help them keep their change leadership journey alive.

Display PowerPoint slide 7–48, citing Lau Tzu's approach to leadership as someone who enables others to accomplish great things.

Thank them for their active participation in the full-day and now the half-day session. Encourage them to contact you if they have questions about change leadership in the future.

11:55   Evaluation (5 minutes)

Display PowerPoint slide 7–49. Thank the participants for attending the Leading Change Follow-Up Workshop and for their active involvement throughout the session. Distribute the training program evaluation form and encourage participants to leave the completed forms at their tables or at a designated location.

Noon   Close

What to Do Next

- ◆ Prepare for the one-day session.

- ◆ Decide whether to offer the half-day follow-up workshop.

- ◆ Compile the learning activities, handouts, and PowerPoint slides you will use in the training.

◆ ◆ ◆

The next chapter includes an agenda and learning activities for a change leadership training workshop for employees.

Training Instrument 7–1

Reflections on Leading Change

Instructions: Reflect on the results and outcomes from your change leadership efforts since the Leading Change Workshop for Managers and Supervisors as you answer the following questions:

1. **What has worked?** What about your efforts to introduce, lead, and sustain changes in your area has worked? What has gone well? What positive results are you seeing or experiencing?

2. **What hasn't worked?** What about your efforts to introduce, lead, and sustain changes in your area has *not* worked? What has not gone as well as you had planned or hoped? What are some of the less than desirable results that you are seeing or experiencing?

3. **Why has it worked or not worked?** What enabled you to achieve the change results you had hoped for? What prevented you from achieving positive results (if you didn't)?

4. **What will you do differently in the near future?** What actions will you take to improve your successes at introducing and sustaining change? What will you do more or less of to increase employee and other stakeholder commitment to the change?

5. **What still confuses and frustrates you about your role and responsibility in introducing change?** What isn't clear? What methods or models are still fuzzy?

Training Instrument 7–2
Next Steps for Leading Change

Instructions: What are the next steps you can take to help move yourself and others toward commitment to the change? Reflect on our discussions as you develop your plan for moving your team or workgroup out of Comfort and Control and Fear, Anger, and Resistance; through Inquiry, Experimentation, and Discovery; and toward Learning, Acceptance, and Commitment.

Specific actions I will take to sustain commitment to the change and other changes include

1. _____

2. _____

3. _____

4. _____

5. _____

6. _____

Slide 7–1

Welcome to . . .

Leading Change

*Strategies for Guiding and Motivating
People during Turbulent Times*

Slide 7–2

Your Perceptions of Change

What are your reactions when you
hear the word "change"?

- Negative perceptions
- Positive perceptions

Slide 7–3

Today's Agenda . . . Morning

- Perceptions of Change
- Why We're Here . . . Today's Learning Goals and Objectives
- Experiencing Personal Change
- A Model for Understanding the Human Responses to Change
- Actions for Introducing/Leading Change

Slide 7–4

Today's Agenda . . . Afternoon

- The Forces Causing Change
- Understanding Change Resistance
- Identifying the Perceived Losses and Opportunities from Change
- Developing Change Resilience in Yourself and Others

Slide 7–5

In Your Small Group . . .

Exploring your goals and questions:

First . . .

- Select a group leader.
- Meet and greet.

Then . . .

- Share your personal objectives.
- Develop two or three questions that your group would like to have answered by the end of this workshop.

Slide 7–6

Experiencing Personal Change

1. Before you knew the change was coming or needed . . .

2. In the earliest days of the change . . . when you are beginning to feel the effects of the change . . .

3. After the change is half-way complete . . .

4. After the change is complete . . . when you're looking back on the path you've followed . . .

Slide 7–7

In Your Small Group . . .

- Discuss common reactions, thoughts, and feelings for each of the four journal entries.
- Discuss whether being "locked in the trunk" or having "a hand on the wheel" made a difference in how change was perceived.
- Discuss whether a change being perceived as negative or positive made a difference in how people responded.
- Discuss whether the change being personal or professional made a difference in how people responded.

Slide 7–8

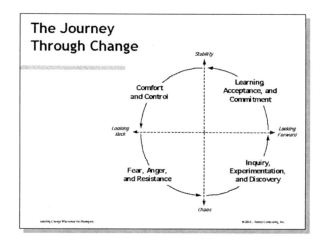

The Journey Through Change

Slide 7–9

Characteristics of *Comfort and Control*

- Comfortable
- Safe
- Everything's fine
- Happy
- Satisfied
- No problems
- Positive
- Rewarding
- In control
- I'm okay, you're okay!

People feel comfortable, safe, and in control. They are working hard – but often on the wrong things.

Slide 7–10

Characteristics of *Fear, Anger, and Resistance*

- Frustration
- Anger
- Fearful
- Betrayed
- Upset
- Confused
- Challenged
- Hostility
- Anxiety
- Self-doubt
- Lost
- Dazed

People feel frustrated, angry, and fearful about the change. Performance deteriorates.

Slide 7–11

Characteristics of *Inquiry, Experimentation, and Discovery*

- Confused
- Questioning
- Hopeful
- Opportunity
- Frustrated
- Disappointed
- Challenged
- Half-way there!
- Making progress
- Going in all directions at once!
- Searching for solutions
- Exciting!
- Innovation/creativity

People want to make the change work – on their terms as well as those of the organization – but they don't have clear answers.

Slide 7–12

Characteristics of *Learning, Acceptance, and Commitment*

- Now I know!
- Energized
- Success!
- We made it!
- Relief
- Wow!
- Self-confidence
- Satisfied
- Comfortable
- What's next?

People are focused on and excited about the future. They begin working together to accomplish the change vision.

Slide 7–13

Getting Stuck in the Journey

When people get stuck here . . .	→ It can lead to this . . .
Comfort and Control	→ Complacency and Obsolescence
Fear, Anger, and Resistance	→ Sickness and Depression
Inquiry, Experimentation, and Discovery	→ Anxiety and Lack of Integration
Learning, Acceptance, and Commitment	→ Gradual Drift "Backward" into Comfort and Control

Slide 7–14

In Your Small Group . . .

What specific actions can we take to help
- ourselves
- others

along the emotional journey through change?

Slide 7–15

Actions for *Comfort and Control*

- Acknowledge their successful past.
- Get people's attention!
- Sell the need for change . . . sell the pain and the consequences of not changing.
- Immerse people in information about the change . . . customer complaints, budget data, increasing costs, competitive pressures.
- Let people know it will happen— one way or another!
- Give people time to let the ideas sink in.
- Don't sell the solutions . . . sell the problem!

Slide 7–16

Actions for *Fear, Anger, and Resistance*

- Co-create the vision.
- Listen, listen, listen.
- Acknowledge people's pain, perceived losses, and anger.
- Strive to address their perceived losses.
- Tell people what you know— and what you don't know.
- Don't try to talk people out of their feelings.
- Discuss ways to *solve* the problems people see with the change.
- Encourage discussion, dissent, disagreement, debate . . . keep people talking

Slide 7–17

Actions for *Inquiry, Experimentation, and Discovery*

- Give people freedom and direction.
- Give people permission to find their own solutions.
- Encourage people to take risks.
- Affirm and refine the vision— make room for others' ideas.
- Tell people as much as you know.
- Encourage teamwork/collaboration.
- Encourage personal reflection and learning.
- Provide people with training and support.
- Set short-term goals.

Slide 7–18

Actions for *Learning, Acceptance, and Commitment*

- Acknowledge their hard work.
- Celebrate successes and accomplishments.
- Reaffirm the vision.
- Bring people together toward the vision.
- Acknowledge what people have left behind.
- Develop long-term goals and plans.
- Provide tools and training to reinforce new behaviors.
- Reinforce and reward the new behaviors.
- Create systems/structures that reinforce new behaviors.
- Prepare people for the next change.

Slide 7–19

Leader Actions . . .

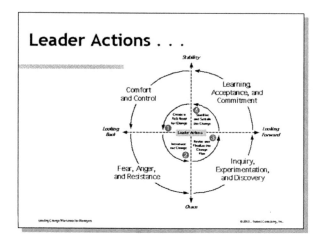

Slide 7–20

In Your Small Group . . .

What specific actions can we take to introduce, lead, and sustain a specific change in our organization?

Identify actions that help you

- Initiate or introduce the change.
- Respond to the emotional needs of people at the respective stage.
- Meet the noted "key challenge."

Slide 7–21

Create a Felt Need

- Identify what needs to change.
- Identify *why* it must change – identify the problem that needs to be solved.
- Immerse them in the data from the customer, from other stakeholders, from the organization's performance successes and failures.
- Identify the *consequences* for the organization of <u>not</u> solving the problem or <u>not</u> responding to the challenge.
- Get their attention – give people a reason to move out of comfort and complacency.

Slide 7–22

Introduce the Change

- Ask people to solve the "problem."
- Offer your own possible solutions and strategies.
- Work with others to co-create a shared change vision.
- Guide people in exploring the positive outcomes.
- Listen to people's objections, concerns, fears, and perceived losses.
- Acknowledge their fears and perceived losses.
- Invite people to offer ideas to offset the losses and realize the benefits.
- Integrate their concerns about and ideas for improving change.

Slide 7–23

Revise and Finalize the Change

- Help people
  - identify/explore the hidden opportunities
  - define the future of the change on their terms and those of the organization
  - invent creative solutions to the challenges
- Continue to identify obstacles to change acceptance that must be overcome – explore the hidden opportunities.
- Encourage people to find creative answers to their questions about the change.
- Adjust the change vision, strategy, and plan in response to the ideas and answers offered by stakeholders.

Slide 7–24

Stabilize and Sustain the Change

- Develop action steps for stabilizing, reinforcing, and sustaining the change:
  - Give people time to mourn their actual losses
  - Provide skill and knowledge training
  - Revise job descriptions
  - Develop new reward systems
  - Strengthen social connections and relationships
  - Recognize and celebrate accomplishments
- Develop performance measures to evaluate the results from the change.
- Make adjustments to the change vision and strategy to reflect new learning and insights.
- Challenge people to be open to new challenges, forces, and pressures for the next change.

Slide 7–25

The art of progress is to
preserve change amid order and
preserve order amid change.

— Alfred North Whitehead
British mathematician and
philosopher (1861-1947)

Slide 7–26

The Forces for Change . . .

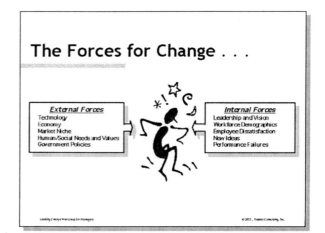

Slide 7–27

Exploring the Forces . . .

First, by <u>yourself</u> . . . Identify the external and
internal forces for change that you see putting
pressure on this organization. . . .

Then, as a <u>group</u>:

✓ Discuss your individual lists.

✓ Explore agreement on the key forces.

✓ Identify the consequences if the
organization doesn't respond
effectively to these forces.

Slide 7–28

Responding to the Forces . . .

For each key force pressuring the
organization to change, identify at least
<u>three</u> constructive ways in which the
organization can
respond effectively.

Slide 7–29

Change
is inevitable,
growth is optional

Slide 7–30

There is nothing more delicate to take in
hand, nor more dangerous to conduct, nor
more doubtful of success, than to step up
as a leader in the introduction of changes.

For he who innovates will have for his
enemies all those who are well off under
the existing order of things, and only
lukewarm supporters in those who might
be better off under the new.

— Niccolò Machiavelli
The Prince, 1527

Slide 7–31

The Origins of Resistance . . .

- Some people fear loss.
- Some people mistrust those who lead.
- Some people disagree on the change.
- Some people don't tolerate change well.

Slide 7–32

In Your Small Group . . .

- Which of the reasons for change resistance are the most likely causes of resistance in this organization or for this change?
- Identify at least two or three actions that change leaders and those affected by the change can take to help reduce or eliminate that source of resistance.

Slide 7–33

We Value Resisters Because . . .

- They clarify the problem.
- They identify other problems that need to be solved first.
- They force change leaders to think before they implement the change.
- Their tough questions can strengthen and improve the change.
- They let us know who opposes the change.
- They slow down the change.
- They may be right, it is a dumb idea!

Slide 7–34

The Crisis of Change . . .

Danger!

Hidden Opportunity

Slide 7–35

The PERCEIVED Losses . . .

- Job Security
- Psychological Comfort and Security
- Control over One's Future
- Purpose/Meaning
- Competence
- Social Connections

- Territory
- Future Opportunities
- Power
- Social Status
- Trust in Others
- Independence and Autonomy

Of these potential losses, which are people most likely to experience from the coming changes?

What can we do to reduce or eliminate these losses?

Slide 7–36

In Your Small Group . . .

- Discuss the most likely perceived losses from the change.
- Identify at least two or three actions people can take to reduce, eliminate, or offset the perceived loss with a hidden opportunity.

Slide 7–37

Human Nature . . .

- People want to maintain control over their lives.
- People develop self-confidence and psychological health by building stable and effective relationships with others.
- Our sense of control, comfort, and well-being results from the degree of certainty we have about our life and our future.
- Change disrupts our ability to predict whats in store for us.
- The more a change disrupts our ability to envision our future, the greater our confusion, fear, anxiety, and self-doubt.

Slide 7–38

Resilience is . . .

- The ability to recover from or adjust easily to misfortune or change.

- The capability of a strained body to recover its size and shape after being subjected to adversity or stress.

Slide 7–39

Develop Your *Resilience*

- Self-Assured
- Clarity of Personal Vision
- Flexible
- Organized
- Problem Solver
- Interpersonal Competence
- Socially Connected
- Proactive

Slide 7–40

In Your Small Group . . .

- Discuss your reactions to and questions about resilience and its dimensions.

- Identify three or four actions that leaders and individuals can take generally to develop and strengthen resilience in themselves and others.

Slide 7–41

Blessed are the flexible, for they shall not be bent out of shape.

— Dr. Michael McGriffy

Slide 7–42

Thank You!!

- Please complete the workshop evaluation.

- Good luck with your change leadership!

Slide 7–43

Welcome to . . .

Follow-Up Leading Change Workshop

Reviewing and Reflecting on Your Change Leadership Progress

Slide 7–44

Today's Agenda . . .

- Review the leading change model.
- Answer questions about the integrated model for leading change.
- Discuss your progress in helping people through change.
- Identify additional steps you can take to enhance your change leadership abilities.

Slide 7–45

In Your Small Group . . .

First . . .
- Select a group leader.
- Meet and greet.

Then . . .
- Discuss what worked and what didn't work with your leading change efforts.
- Discuss what remains unclear or confusing about your responsibilities and roles for leading change.
- Develop two or three questions that your group would like to have answered about leading change, your roles in it, and the models explored at the day-long workshop.

Slide 7–46

The Integrated Change Leadership Model . . .

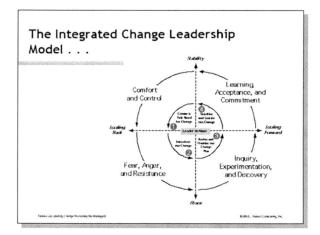

Slide 7–47

In Your Small Group . . .

- Select a new group leader.
- Develop a response to your assigned question(s).

Slide 7–48

The master doesn't talk, he acts. When his work is done, the people say "Amazing! We did it all by ourselves."

— Lao-Tzu
Author of *Tao Te Ching*
500 BC

Slide 7–49

Thank You!!

- Please complete the workshop evaluation.

- Good luck with your change leadership!

Workshops for Employees

What's in This Chapter?

- Objectives, materials, and step-by-step preparations for the one-day Leading Change Workshop for Employees

- Objectives, materials, and step-by-step preparations for the half-day Follow-Up Workshop for Employees

- Sample one-day and half-day workshop agendas

- PowerPoint slides for the workshops

The people who most often are affected by change and those who end up having to implement change are an organization's employees. These are the people who contribute their ideas, energy, and labor to create value for the organization every day. For this reason, any successful organizational change strategy must develop employee competencies that involve an understanding of the forces that are causing change, a knowledge of the emotional impact of change on themselves and others, and an awareness of the qualities of personal resilience in the face of organizational change.

This chapter presents a one-day workshop that is designed to develop these critical employee understandings and skills. It seeks to help employees not only to realize a positive result through an organizational change but also to enable them to offer constructive ideas and suggestions that can contribute to improving the change itself. An additional half-day follow-up workshop is offered to help integrate, reinforce, and enhance participant learning from the one-day workshop.

Although the session is designed to focus on the concerns, problems, and responsibilities of employees (as opposed to managers and executives), we strongly encourage you to have managers and supervisors attend and partici-pate in the session. Although many aspects of the training program design echo those of the Leading Change Workshop for Managers and Supervisors (chapter 7), it is important that managers and supervisors attend the general employee session, both to hear employee issues and concerns regarding the proposed changes and to participate in the discussion of employee ideas for improving the change plan and strategy.

Although some trainers might be concerned that including managers and su-pervisors in the employee workshop on leading change will be intimidating to employees, our experience has been otherwise. We believe that, in most cases, the risk of intimidation is significantly offset by the gains realized by bringing people together, listening to each other and working together to find a path toward change commitment. Each trainer needs to make his or her own judgment as to the impact of managers and supervisors being present. Generally, we strive for integration, but there are cases when the level of fear in an organization is such that separating managers and supervisors from em-ployees would facilitate a better learning environment.

For some employees, however, the presence of a supervisor or managers will always create some discomfort. The trainer can help reduce this anxiety that some may feel by establishing ground rules at the beginning of a training ses-sion (to help create a safe environment), by ensuring that employees aren't placed in the same table group as their supervisors and managers, or by hav-ing supervisors and managers work in their own table group.

One-Day Leading Change Workshop for Employees

TRAINING OBJECTIVES

The objectives of the Leading Change Workshop for Employees are to

- ◆ recognize the impact that change has on employees and how it might affect customers and other stakeholders

- ◆ identify the actions people can take to enable a healthy response to change

- ◆ describe the forces causing organizational change and the implica-tions for the organization

◆ identify the losses and hidden opportunities created by the change

◆ develop resilience in those affected by the change.

MATERIALS

For the instructor:

◆ Learning Activity 9–1: Perceptions of Change

◆ Learning Activity 9–2: Experiencing Personal Change

◆ Learning Activity 9–3: Guiding People through the Change Journey

◆ Learning Activity 9–5: The Forces Causing Change

◆ Learning Activity 9–6: The Sources of Change Resistance

◆ Learning Activity 9–7: Identifying the Perceived Losses and Exploring the Opportunities from a Proposed Change

◆ Learning Activity 9–8: Strengthening Change Resilience

◆ Tool 10–1: Training Room Configuration/Layout

◆ Tool 10–2: Ah Ha! Sheet

◆ Tool 10–3: Goal-Setting Worksheet

◆ Tool 10–4: Sample Training Program Evaluation

◆ Flipchart and marking pens

◆ Flipchart page labeled "Parking Lot"

◆ PowerPoint slides 8–1 through 8–37. To access slides for this program, open the file *Leading Change–Employees.ppt* on the accompanying CD. Reference copies of the slides for this training session are included at the end of this chapter.

For the participants:

◆ Training Instrument 9–1: Perceptions of Change

◆ Training Instrument 9–2: Experiencing Personal Change

◆ Training Instrument 9–3: Characteristics of and Actions for Each Phase of the Change Journey

- Training Instrument 9–4: Personal Plan for Helping Yourself and Others through Change

- Training Instrument 9–7: The Forces Causing Change

- Training Instrument 9–8: Responding to the Forces for Change

- Training Instrument 9–9: The Origins of Change Resistance

- Training Instrument 9–10: Personal Plan for Dealing with Change Resistance

- Training Instrument 9–11: Experiencing the Losses of Change

- Training Instrument 9–12: Personal Plan for Action: Dealing with the Perceived Losses

- Training Instrument 9–13: Characteristics of Change Resilience

- Training Instrument 9–15: Personal Plan for Strengthening Your Resilience

- Handout 9–1: The Journey through Change

- Handout 9–2: Actions for Guiding People through Change

- Handout 9–3: An Integrated Model for Leading Change

- Handout 9–5: Why We Value Change Resisters

- Handout 9–6: The Crisis of Change

- Handout 9–7: Human Nature and the Character of Change

- Tool 10–2: Ah Ha! Sheet

- Tool 10–3: Goal-Setting Worksheet

PREPARATIONS

Before the workshop:

- Meet with a representative or representatives of the executive leadership group to discuss their change initiative and to explore the implications of the change on employees throughout the organization.

- Schedule the session and secure a training room for the one-day workshop. If the half-day follow-up workshop detailed in this chapter is planned, schedule this session and room at the same time.

◆ Design the program around the proposed change initiative, the priorities of the executive group (or the group that is initiating the change), and the likely impact of the change on employees at all levels of the organization.

◆ Prepare training materials (handouts, training instruments, tools, instructions, training program evaluation form, PowerPoint presentation, and supporting audiovisual materials).

◆ Send a memo, letter, or email of invitation to participants, reiterating the purpose of the Leading Change Workshop for Employees and the importance of the workshop in helping them deal more effectively with the coming changes.

◆ Order food and beverages as necessary.

Just prior to the workshop:

◆ Arrive early at the training room.

◆ Verify room setup.

◆ Set up and test such equipment as flipchart, markers, LCD projector, or overhead projector.

◆ Prepare and post flipchart pages titled "Your Goals/Questions" and "Parking Lot," and additional flipchart pages as detailed in the learning activities. You may also want to post another flipchart page highlighting key questions that relate to the objectives that will be addressed during the workshop.

◆ Place materials on tables.

◆ Display PowerPoint slide 8–1 as a welcome and greeting to participants as they enter the training room.

◆ Greet participants individually as they enter the training room.

SAMPLE AGENDA: LEADING CHANGE WORKSHOP FOR EMPLOYEES

8:30 a.m. Welcome (5 minutes)

Welcome participants to the Leading Change Workshop for Employees, introduce yourself, highlight the main purpose of the workshop, and emphasize the importance of this session as a key step in helping them better understand the reasons behind the coming changes and how they can better take care of themselves throughout those changes.

8:35 Learning Activity 9–1: Perceptions of Change (chapter 9, page 133) (10 minutes)

Display PowerPoint slide 8–2 and facilitate Learning Activity 9–1. This activity quickly gets participants to begin reflecting on their positive and negative perceptions of change and begins the dialogue about why people may resist change initiatives.

8:45 Goal Setting (30 minutes)

Make the transition from the previous activity by linking the exploration of why people might end up in the "negative" column and the importance of using the time in this workshop to find ways to help create positive outcomes from the change initiatives.

Review the specific goals and roadmap for the day with PowerPoint slides 8–3 and 8–4.

Distribute Tool 10–3: Goal-Setting Worksheet (chapter 10, page 187). Ask participants to identify

◆ their personal objectives for the workshop and how likely it is that they will realize these objectives through this training session

◆ what's in it for them if they achieve their objective and how likely it is that this "reward" will occur

◆ how important this positive benefit or reward is to them.

After a couple of minutes, display PowerPoint slide 8–5 and ask participants to work in their small groups to (a) meet and greet; (b) share their personal objectives (the first of the questions on the Goal-Setting Worksheet); and (c) identify, as a group, two or three questions about leading change that the group would like to address during the workshop. Give the small groups approximately seven minutes for this activity.

Have the groups report their questions and record these on the prepared flipchart page. Highlight the importance of the attendees taking responsibility for their own learning by seeking out the answers to these questions as they work their way through the workshop.

Indicate that you have posted a "Parking Lot" (flipchart page) as a place to record additional issues and questions that you may not be able to address today. Encourage them to identify these "parking lot" concerns at any time to ensure that the issue is identified for future consideration.

Distribute Tool 10–2: Ah Ha! Sheet (chapter 10, page 185). Emphasize the importance of their making notes on this Ah Ha! Sheet throughout the day, based upon what they hear, see, and learn. Encourage them to be active participants in their own learning by using the Ah Ha! Sheet to record the key learning moments and insights that will be most useful to them beyond today's session.

Note the schedule for breaks and lunch, and the location of restrooms, telephones, and refreshments.

9:15   Learning Activity 9–2: Experiencing Personal Change (chapter 9, page 123) (50 minutes)

Guide participants through this activity to help them see the pattern in their emotional response to change.

10:05   Break (15 minutes)

10:20   Learning Activity 9–3: Guiding People through the Change Journey (chapter 9, page 134) (50 minutes)

This activity helps participants understand how they can ease their own journeys through change, as well as those of others.

11:10   Introducing a Change (5 minutes)

Display PowerPoint slide 8–19 and distribute Handout 9–7. Present a brief overview of the responsibilities of

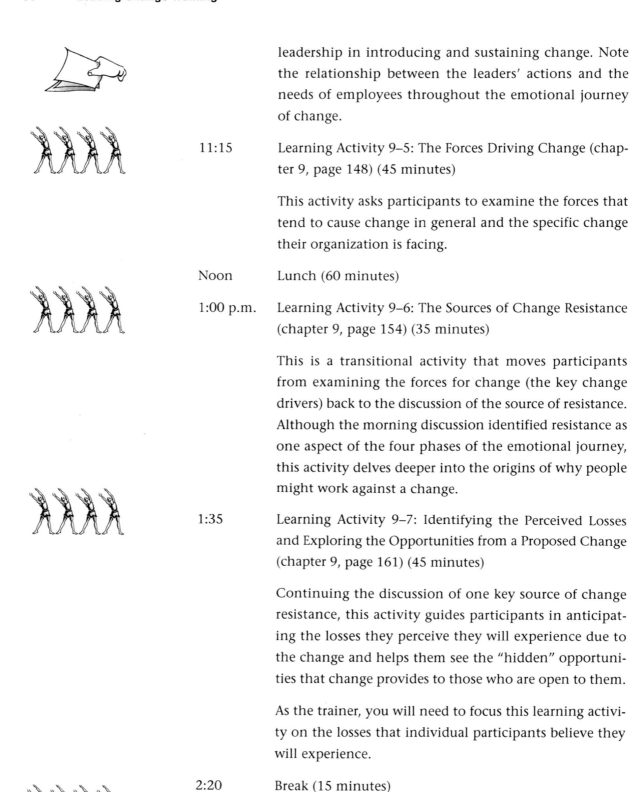

leadership in introducing and sustaining change. Note the relationship between the leaders' actions and the needs of employees throughout the emotional journey of change.

11:15   Learning Activity 9–5: The Forces Driving Change (chapter 9, page 148) (45 minutes)

This activity asks participants to examine the forces that tend to cause change in general and the specific change their organization is facing.

Noon   Lunch (60 minutes)

1:00 p.m.   Learning Activity 9–6: The Sources of Change Resistance (chapter 9, page 154) (35 minutes)

This is a transitional activity that moves participants from examining the forces for change (the key change drivers) back to the discussion of the source of resistance. Although the morning discussion identified resistance as one aspect of the four phases of the emotional journey, this activity delves deeper into the origins of why people might work against a change.

1:35   Learning Activity 9–7: Identifying the Perceived Losses and Exploring the Opportunities from a Proposed Change (chapter 9, page 161) (45 minutes)

Continuing the discussion of one key source of change resistance, this activity guides participants in anticipating the losses they perceive they will experience due to the change and helps them see the "hidden" opportunities that change provides to those who are open to them.

As the trainer, you will need to focus this learning activity on the losses that individual participants believe they will experience.

2:20   Break (15 minutes)

2:35   Learning Activity 9–8: Strengthening Change Resilience (chapter 9, page 169) (45 minutes)

The final module of the Leading Change Workshop for Employees introduces the concept of resilience—the human capacity to spring back in the face of adversity. The activity also guides participants in strengthening their own resilience.

3:20   Integration and Conclusion (35 minutes)

Tie together the various elements of the workshop content and review the questions the group identified earlier in the day in the goal-setting segment. Ask participants to answer any question that has not yet been addressed during the workshop. Depending upon time available, you can either assign these questions to the small groups or facilitate a group discussion of them.

In conclusion, emphasize that in the face of change, people have a choice. They can resist the change and experience the negative personal side effects of resistance or they make the change work for them. This doesn't mean that every change is always good for everyone, but it does mean that they each have a choice in how they respond to it: They can get sick or they can actively approach the change and seek out the hidden opportunities.

If the half-day follow-up workshop is planned, remind the attendees of the date of the session and of their assignment for that session.

3:55   Evaluation (5 minutes)

Display PowerPoint slide 8–37. Thank the participants for attending the Leading Change Workshop and for their active involvement throughout the session. Distribute the training program evaluation form and encourage participants to leave the completed forms at their tables or at a designated location.

4:00   Close

Half-Day Follow-Up Leading Change Workshop for Employees

TRAINING OBJECTIVES

The objectives of the half-day Follow-Up Leading Change Workshop for Employees are

- to discuss progress the participants are making in responding to the change

- to identify employee suggestions for proactively improving the change ideas and the implementation strategy and plan.

MATERIALS

For the instructor:

- Flipchart and marking pens

- PowerPoint slides 8–38 through 8–45.

PREPARATIONS

Before the workshop:

- Schedule the session and secure a training room prior to offering the initial one-day workshop for employees.

- Decide on the learning objectives for the session. If you are facilitating this workshop based on a specific change or set of changes in the organization, then you will likely address both learning objectives and offer the entire half-day workshop. If, however, the workshop is addressing non-specific changes in the organization, you may choose to focus on only the first learning objective and offer only the first half of the workshop (up to the 10:10 break), ending the workshop with Integration and Close.

  Prepare training materials (handouts, training instruments, tools, instructions, training program evaluation form, PowerPoint presentation, and supporting audiovisual materials). The PowerPoint presentation slides that accompany the Follow-Up Leading Change Workshop for Employees are located on the CD as *Follow-Up (Employees).ppt.*

Send a follow-up memo, letter, or email to participants in the full-day Leading Change Workshop for Employees, reminding them of the half-day follow-up session and reiterating what they should be working on and should be prepared to discuss and share at the follow-up session. Ask participants to bring copies of their materials from the full-day session.

◆ Order food and beverages as necessary.

Just prior to the workshop:

◆ Arrive early at the training room.

◆ Verify room setup.

◆ Set up and test such equipment as flipchart, markers, LCD projector, or overhead projector. You may wish to provide a flipchart easel with paper for each of the small-group tables. These flipcharts may be used by the groups in reporting their answers to questions assigned to them during the session.

◆ Prepare and post three flipchart pages titled "Your Goals/Questions," "Parking Lot," and "Ideas for Improving the Change Plan."

◆ Place materials on tables.

◆ Display PowerPoint 8–38 as a "Welcome Back" greeting to participants as they enter the training room.

◆ Greet participants individually as they enter the training room.

SAMPLE AGENDA: FOLLOW-UP LEADING CHANGE WORKSHOP FOR EMPLOYEES

8:30 a.m. Welcome (5 minutes)

Welcome returning participants to the follow-up session to the Leading Change Workshop for Employees. Display PowerPoint slide 8–39 as you highlight the purpose and goals of the follow-up workshop and emphasize the importance of this follow-up session as an opportunity to continue to address questions and issues regarding the coming changes. Note that the "Parking Lot" (from the one-day session) is available and can be added to as new issues and questions emerge during this session.

8:35   Reflection on Personal Responses to Change
(35 minutes)

Ask participants to work by themselves for five minutes to reflect upon their experience with and reactions to the changes that have occurred before and since the initial leading change workshop.

Reconvene the large group. Display PowerPoint slide 8–40 and ask people to meet in their small groups to (a) select a group leader, (b) meet and greet, (c) discuss reactions to the changes taking place in the organization, (d) review the actions that they have taken to strengthen their re-silience and become more proactive in shaping the change, and (e) develop two or three questions about change that their group would like to have answered dur-ing this half-day workshop. Give the small groups 8 to 10 minutes for this.

Facilitate a large group discussion of their reactions to the changes and the actions they have already taken to strengthen their resilience and become more proactive in shaping the change. Guide the groups in identifying questions on which they would like to focus during this half-day follow-up workshop. Record the questions on the prepared flipchart page.

Indicate that much of the time in this workshop will fo-cus on exploring answers to their questions and in offer-ing ideas and suggestions for improving the organiza-tion's change vision, strategy, and plan.

Facilitator Note: After the group members offer their ques-tions, you may want to identify which questions are best answered by you, by the participants themselves, or by parties not present, such as the executive change leader-ship group (change design team) or other parties not present. You can invite the group to help you sort these questions by who might be in the best position to pro-vide useful answers.

After you have personally reflected upon the questions (or asked the group to help you do this), point out that some of these questions may be best answered by people not present at the workshop and suggest that these can be added to the Parking Lot for future consideration and response by the appropriate party.

9:10   Review of the Integrated Change Leadership Model
(10 minutes)

Display PowerPoint slide 8–41. Offer a quick review of the two change processes occurring at the same time: the inner circle reflects the actions of change leaders; the outer circle reflects the emotional journey that people follow.

Note that people have legitimate issues and concerns as change is introduced. Indicate that change leaders have a clear responsibility to understand the impact of these changes on others and those who are affected by the change have a responsibility to take care of themselves while responding proactively to the change ideas.

9:20   Exploring Questions and Issues about the Change
(50 minutes)

Select the questions about change that seem most appropriate for the groups to answer themselves. Assign one or two questions to each of the groups, taking care not to ask a group to answer its own question. You may want to assign some questions to more than one group or, if a question seems critically important, assign it to all of the groups. (*Note:* You might find it useful and provocative to assign to the groups some of the change-specific questions that either you or the group earlier decided would best be answered by people not present.)

Display PowerPoint slide 8–42. Ask the groups to select a leader and give the groups 10 to 15 minutes to develop answers to their assigned questions. If desired, you can direct the groups to write their recommended answers on flipchart paper that you have made available.

While the small groups are developing their answers, develop possible responses to questions that are best for you to answer.

As time permits, check on each group's progress and provide clarification and direction as necessary.

Once the groups have developed responses to their assigned questions, facilitate the process of the groups' reporting their suggested answers. Offer responses to questions that you agreed to answer. For questions about the change that neither you nor the participants are able to answer, highlight the process for addressing the specific Parking Lot questions about the change with those not attending.

10:10   Break (15 minutes)

10:25   Ideas and Suggestions for Improving the Change Vision and Plan (80 minutes)

Make the transition to this activity by noting that, so far, the session has explored issues and questions about the coming changes and the impact of these changes on them as individuals. Suggest that the balance of the workshop will focus on offering specific ideas and suggestions for improving the change vision and strategy itself.

Display PowerPoint slide 8–43. Ask participants to work in small groups to select a group leader and then to identify specific ideas and suggestions for improving the planned change or changes. If there are multiple changes being implemented by the organization, invite the individual groups to select a specific change or set of interrelated changes and to develop a list of specific ideas and suggestions for improving the change results (vision), strategy, or plan. Ask the groups to write their change improvement ideas and suggestions on flipchart paper. Give the groups approximately 30 minutes to complete this activity.

After 30 minutes, ask the groups to share their change improvement ideas and suggestions.

Facilitate the reporting of the change ideas and suggestions. If desired, record ideas and suggestions themes identified by the group on a flipchart page for future reference.

Record additional issues at the Parking Lot as required.

11:45   Integration (10 minutes)

Thank participants for their active involvement in the follow-up session. Indicate that their involvement in exploring the issues concerning the changes facing the organization is an important step in strengthening their resilience and in making the change work for rather than against them.

Identify what will be done with the change improvement ideas and suggestions they have offered. If any ideas, suggestions, or Parking Lot ideas require a follow-up with participants, indicate how this will occur and when.

Display PowerPoint slide 8–44. Suggest that personal responsibility is what enables people to be most resilient and to become strong in spite of what change and the world throws at them.

11:55   Evaluation (5 minutes)

Display PowerPoint slide 8–45. Thank the participants for attending the Leading Change Workshop and for their active involvement throughout the session. Distribute the training program evaluation form and encourage participants to leave the completed forms at their tables or at a designated location.

What to Do Next

◆ Prepare for the one-day session.

◆ Decide on whether to offer the half-day follow-up workshop.

◆ Decide on the learning objectives for the half-day follow-up session.

- Compile the learning activities, handouts, and PowerPoint slides you will use in the training.

◆ ◆ ◆

The next chapter presents all of the learning activities used in the workshops developed in chapters 6 through 8.

Slide 8–1

Welcome to . . .

Leading Change

*Strategies for Helping Yourself and
Others through Change*

Slide 8–2

Your Perceptions of Change

What are your reactions when
you hear the word "change"?

■ Negative perceptions

■ Positive perceptions

Slide 8–3

Today's Agenda . . . Morning

- ■ Perceptions of Change
- ■ Why We're Here . . . Today's Learning Goals and Objectives
- ■ Experiencing Personal Change
- ■ A Model for Understanding the Human Responses to Change
- ■ The Forces Driving Change

Slide 8–4

Today's Agenda . . . Afternoon

- ■ Understanding Change Resistance
- ■ Identifying the Perceived Losses and Opportunities from Change
- ■ Developing Change Resilience in Yourself and Others

Slide 8–5

In Your Small Group . . .

Exploring your goals and questions:

First . . .

- ■ Select a group leader.
- ■ Meet and greet.

Then . . .

- ■ Share your personal objectives.
- ■ Develop two or three questions that your group would like to have answered by the end of this workshop.

Slide 8–6

Experiencing Personal Change

1. Before you knew the change was coming or needed . . .

2. In the earliest days of the change . . . when you are beginning to feel the effects of the change . . .

3. After the change is half-way complete . . .

4. After the change is complete . . . when you're looking back on the path you've followed . . .

Slide 8–7

In Your Small Group . . .

- Discuss common reactions, thoughts, and feelings for each of the four journal entries.
- Discuss whether being "locked in the trunk" or having "a hand on the wheel" made a difference in how change was perceived.
- Discuss whether a change being perceived as negative or positive made a difference in how people responded.
- Discuss whether the change being personal or professional made a difference in how people responded.

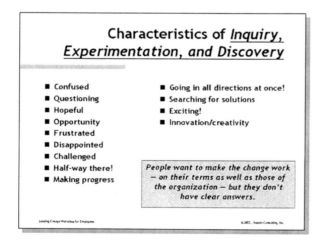

Slide 8–8

The Journey Through Change

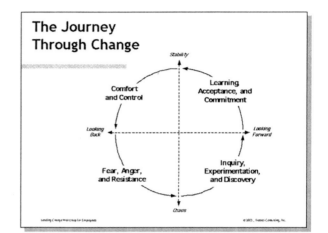

Slide 8–9

Characteristics of *Comfort and Control*

- Comfortable
- Safe
- Everything's fine
- Happy
- Satisfied
- No problems
- Positive
- Rewarding
- In control
- I'm okay, you're okay!

People feel comfortable, safe, and in control. They are working hard – but often on the wrong things.

Slide 8–10

Characteristics of *Fear, Anger, and Resistance*

- Frustration
- Anger
- Fearful
- Betrayed
- Upset
- Confused
- Challenged
- Hostility
- Anxiety
- Self-doubt
- Lost
- Dazed

People feel frustrated, angry, and fearful about the change. Performance deteriorates.

Slide 8–11

Characteristics of *Inquiry, Experimentation, and Discovery*

- Confused
- Questioning
- Hopeful
- Opportunity
- Frustrated
- Disappointed
- Challenged
- Half-way there!
- Making progress
- Going in all directions at once!
- Searching for solutions
- Exciting!
- Innovation/creativity

People want to make the change work – on their terms as well as those of the organization – but they don't have clear answers.

Slide 8–12

Characteristics of *Learning, Acceptance, and Commitment*

- Now I know!
- Energized
- Success!
- We made it!
- Relief
- Wow!
- Self-confidence
- Satisfied
- Comfortable
- What's next?

People are focused on and excited about the future. They begin working together to accomplish the change vision.

Slide 8–13

Getting Stuck in the Journey

When people get stuck here . . .	It can lead to this . . .
Comfort and Control	→ Complacency and Obsolescence
Fear, Anger and Resistance	→ Sickness and Depression
Inquiry, Experimentation, and Discovery	→ Anxiety and Lack of Integration
Learning, Acceptance, and Commitment	→ Gradual Drift "Backward" into Comfort and Control

Leading Change Workshop for Employees   © 2003 , Nusact Consulting, Inc.

Slide 8–14

In Your Small Group . . .

What specific actions can we take to help
- ourselves
- others

along the emotional
journey through change?

Leading Change Workshop for Employees   © 2003 , Nusact Consulting, Inc.

Slide 8–15

Actions for _Comfort and Control_

- Acknowledge their successful past.
- Get people's attention!
- Sell the need for change . . . sell the pain and the consequences of _not_ changing.
- Immerse people in information about the change . . . customer complaints, budget data, increasing costs, competitive pressures.
- Let people know it will happen—one way or another!
- Give people time to let the ideas sink in.
- Don't sell the solutions . . . sell the _problem!_

Leading Change Workshop for Employees   © 2003 , Nusact Consulting, Inc.

Slide 8–16

Actions for _Fear, Anger, and Resistance_

- Co-create the vision.
- Listen, listen, listen.
- Acknowledge people's pain, perceived losses, and anger.
- Strive to address their perceived losses.
- Tell people what you know—and what you _don't_ know.
- Don't try to talk people out of their feelings.
- Discuss ways to _solve_ the problems people see with the change.
- Encourage discussion, dissent, disagreement, debate . . . keep people talking.

Leading Change Workshop for Employees   © 2003 , Nusact Consulting, Inc.

Slide 8–17

Actions for _Inquiry, Experimentation, and Discovery_

- Give people freedom _and_ direction.
- Give people permission to find their own solutions.
- Encourage people to take risks.
- Affirm and refine the vision—make room for others' ideas.
- Tell people as much as you know.
- Encourage teamwork and collaboration.
- Encourage personal reflection and learning.
- Provide people with training and support.
- Set short-term goals.

Leading Change Workshop for Employees   © 2003 , Nusact Consulting, Inc.

Slide 8–18

Actions for _Learning, Acceptance, and Commitment_

- Acknowledge their hard work.
- Celebrate successes and accomplishments.
- Reaffirm the vision.
- Bring people together toward the vision.
- Acknowledge what people have left behind.
- Develop long-term goals and plans.
- Provide tools and training to reinforce new behaviors.
- Reinforce and reward the new behaviors.
- Create systems and structures that reinforce new behaviors.
- Prepare people for the next change.

Leading Change Workshop for Employees   © 2003 , Nusact Consulting, Inc.

Slide 8–19

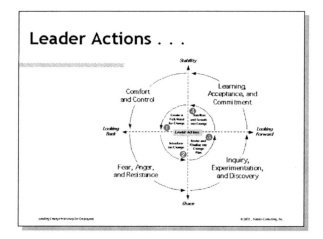

Slide 8–20

The art of progress is to preserve change amid order and preserve order amid change.

— Alfred North Whitehead
British mathematician and philosopher (1861-1947)

Slide 8–21

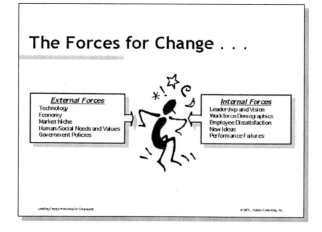

Slide 8–22

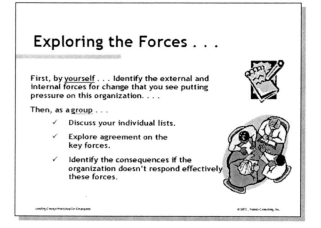

Slide 8–23

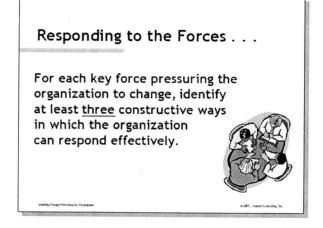

Slide 8–24

Change
is inevitable,
growth is optional

Slide 8–25

There is nothing more delicate to take in hand, nor more dangerous to conduct, nor more doubtful of success, than to step up as a leader in the introduction of changes.

For he who innovates will have for his enemies all those who are well off under the existing order of things, and only lukewarm supporters in those who might be better off under the new.

— Niccolò Machiavelli
The Prince, 1527

Slide 8–26

The Origins of Resistance . . .

- Some people fear loss.
- Some people mistrust those who lead.
- Some people disagree on the change.
- Some people don't tolerate change well.

Slide 8–27

In Your Small Group . . .

- Which of the reasons for change resistance are the most likely causes of resistance in this organization or for this change?
- Identify at least two or three actions that change leaders and those affected by the change can take to help reduce or eliminate that source of resistance.

Slide 8–28

We Value Resisters Because . . .

- They clarify the problem.
- They identify other problems that need to be solved first.
- They force change leaders to think before they implement the change.
- Their tough questions can strengthen and improve the change.
- They let us know who opposes the change.
- They slow down the change.
- They may be right, it is a dumb idea!

Slide 8–29

The Crisis of Change . . .

Danger!

Hidden Opportunity

Slide 8–30

The PERCEIVED Losses . . .

- Job Security
- Psychological Comfort and Security
- Control over One's Future
- Purpose/Meaning
- Competence
- Social Connections

- Territory
- Future Opportunities
- Power
- Social Status
- Trust in Others
- Independence and Autonomy

Of these potential losses, which are people most likely to experience from the coming changes?

What can we do to reduce or eliminate these losses?

Slide 8–31

In Your Small Group . . .

- Discuss the most likely perceived losses from the change.

- Identify at least two or three actions people can take to reduce, eliminate, or offset the perceived loss with a hidden opportunity.

Slide 8–32

Human Nature . . .

- People want to maintain control over their lives.
- People develop self-confidence and psychological health by building stable and effective relationships with others.
- Our sense of control, comfort, and well-being results from the degree of certainty we have about our life and our future.
- Change disrupts our ability to predict whats in store for us.
- The more a change disrupts our ability to envision our future, the greater our confusion, fear, anxiety, and self-doubt.

Slide 8–33

Resilience is . . .

- The ability to recover from or adjust easily to misfortune or change.

- The capability of a strained body to recover its size and shape after being subjected to adversity or stress.

Slide 8–34

Develop Your *Resilience*

- Self-Assured
- Clarity of Personal Vision
- Flexible
- Organized
- Problem Solver
- Interpersonal Competence
- Socially Connected
- Proactive

Slide 8–35

In Your Small Group . . .

- Discuss your reactions to and questions about resilience and its dimensions.

- Identify two or three actions that people can take generally to develop and strengthen resilience in themselves and others.

Slide 8–36

Blessed are the flexible, for they shall not be bent out of shape.

— Dr. Michael McGriffy

Slide 8–37

Thank You!!

- Please complete the workshop evaluation.

- Good luck with the change ahead!

Slide 8–38

Welcome to . . .

Follow-Up Leading Change Workshop

Reviewing and Reflecting on Your Progress with Change

Slide 8–39

Today's Agenda . . .

- Discuss your progress in responding to the changes.

- Identify suggestions for proactively improving the change and the change implementation strategy.

Slide 8–40

In Your Small Group . . .

First . . .
- Select a group leader.
- Meet and greet.

Then . . .
- Discuss reactions to the changes taking place.
- Review the actions you have taken to strengthen your resilience and become more proactive in shaping the change.
- Develop two-three questions about change that your group would like to have answered during this workshop.

Slide 8–41

The Integrated Change Leadership Model . . .

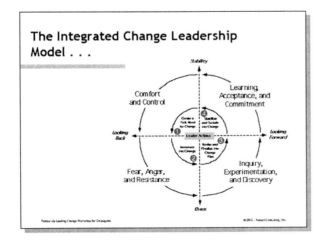

Slide 8–42

In Your Small Group . . .

- Select a new group leader.

- Develop a response to your assigned question(s).

Slide 8–43

In Your Small Group . . .

■ Select a new group leader.

■ Reflect on the changes being implemented. . . . Identify specific ideas and suggestions for improving the planned change or changes.

Slide 8–44

People are always blaming their circumstances for what they are. I don't believe in circumstances. The people who get on in the world are the people who get up and look for the circumstances they want, and if they can't find them, make them.

— George Bernard Shaw
Irish born playwright
(1856-1950)

Slide 8–45

Thank You!!

■ Please complete the workshop evaluation.

■ Good luck with continuing your positive response to change!

Learning Activities

What's in This Chapter?

- Instructions for using the learning activities

- Tips for trainers

- Eight learning activities

- Tools and handouts in support of the learning activities

This chapter presents all of the learning activities identified in the training designs found in chapters 6, 7, and 8. Each learning activity includes the following information:

- **Objectives.** The objectives for each learning activity identify how the activity will help benefit workshop participants. The learning objectives are the primary cognitive, affective, or behavioral outcomes that the activity attempts to achieve.

- **Materials.** Included in the list of materials is everything the trainer will need to successfully conduct that learning activity. A master copy of each handout, training instrument, or tool appears at the end of the activity or can be printed from the appropriate .pdf file on the accompanying CD. For most activities, we recommend that materials be customized to fit the needs of your organization.

- **Time.** An estimated time is offered that defines the period needed to complete the learning activity. This estimate includes introducing the activity, the activity itself, and debriefing and making the transition to the next learning activity.

◆ **Preparations.** This section offers brief instructions on what the trainer or facilitator must do in advance of the activity. Possible advance work includes such things as copying materials, defining a situation or case, preparing flipchart pages, or arranging chairs or tables.

◆ **Instructions.** We provide step-by-step instructions for guiding participants through the activity. Key points you should make, likely reactions or answers from participants, and suggested responses to participant questions are included here. Variations on the activity process and points to make to accommodate different audiences are also here. For example, executives, managers, and employee groups might receive the same activity, but it would be introduced or facilitated differently.

◆ **Debriefing.** The debriefing section guides you in helping participants integrate the activity into their learning. By offering key summary points, posing integrating or synthesizing questions to participants, or guiding participants in action planning, you can significantly strengthen learning and help them make the transition to the next activity.

Using the Accompanying CD

You will find the handouts and tools to which this chapter refers on the CD accompanying this workbook. To access these files, insert the CD and click on the following file names:

◆ Handout [number].pdf

◆ Training Instrument [number].pdf

◆ Tool [number].pdf

The PowerPoint presentation slides that accompany each of the suggested workshops in chapters 6 through 8 are identified on the CD as .ppt files.

To print out the materials for your workshops on leading change, follow these simple steps:

1. Insert the CD into your computer. Your computer should automatically open up a Windows Explorer window that displays a list of all the files on the CD.

2. Locate the handout, training instrument, tool, or PowerPoint file you are looking for and double-click on the file to open it. If the file you are opening is in .pdf format, the document will open using Adobe Acrobat software. If the file you are opening uses the .ppt or .pps format, the document will open in Microsoft PowerPoint.

3. Print out the page or pages of the document(s) that you need for the learning activity and workshop.

In this chapter, the PowerPoint slides to which the learning activities refer are numbered in the order in which they appeared in chapters 6 and 7. You can access individual slides by opening PowerPoint presentations *Executive Briefing.ppt, Leading Change–Managers.ppt, Leading Change–Employees.ppt, Follow-Up (Managers).ppt,* and *Follow-Up (Employees).ppt.*

For additional instructions on using the CD, see the appendix at the end of this workbook.

Tips for Trainers

Designing and delivering top-notch training programs involve blending these suggested workshop agendas, handouts, training instruments, tools, and PowerPoint slides with your own insights, experience, and knowledge. Read and then reread chapter 2 for a broad overview of the change model and process presented in this workbook. The content of this chapter is the very heart of every training program.

Drawing on your own experience and style is an important step toward making these training programs your own. Tell your own stories, use recent events and circumstances, develop your own examples, and identify your organization's cultural myths and legends as you build your customized training programs.

Implementing some or all of the assessment strategies highlighted in chapter 3 in advance of your training design will help ensure that you're on target. Understanding the specific issues, concerns, questions, fears, and perceptions of your executives, managers, and staff is essential as you design each of your programs and shape each learning activity into a meaningful learning experience.

And perhaps most important of all, be flexible. The estimated timeframes offered for each learning activity can and should be changed according to what you learn in your needs assessment, your goals, what stories and examples you have to share, and where you want to focus your energy as a trainer.

As your confidence and competence in delivering the leading change workshops grow and as you receive feedback from participants (using suggestions from chapter 5 on evaluating the training), you will continue to refine and customize your training design. Trust your instincts and your evaluation feedback and make the needed adjustments to your program designs.

Learning Activity 9–1: Perceptions of Change

OBJECTIVES

The objectives of this learning activity are to

- create an initial awareness within participants of the common reactions to change and that these reactions include both positive and negative perceptions

- enable participants to see that experiencing change as either positive or negative results from their response strategies and personalities, as well as the actions of the organization

- challenge participants to explore ways to shift their cognitive, affective, and behavioral responses from the negative to the positive.

MATERIALS

The materials needed for this activity are

- Training Instrument 9–1: Perceptions of Change

- Flipchart and marking pens

- PowerPoint slide 6–3 or 7–2, depending on the workshop.

TIME

- 10 minutes

PREPARATIONS

- Prior to this learning activity, ensure that each participant has a copy of the training instrument.

- Prepare a single flipchart page that closely mirrors Training Instrument 9–1, with the words "Negative" at the top left side of the page and "Positive" at the top right slide. Draw a solid vertical line between the two words, dividing the flip chart page in half.

INSTRUCTIONS

1. Display PowerPoint slide 6–3 or 7–2, depending on the workshop. Distribute Training Instrument 9–1. Ask participants, working by

themselves, to make two lists of words or phrases in reaction to the word "change." Direct them first to jot down negative words or phrases that they think of when they hear the word and then jot down positive words or phrases in response to the word. Give them about two minutes for making their two lists.

2. After two minutes, move toward the prepared flipchart and invite people to offer you examples of words or phrases they wrote down under the negative column. You are likely to hear such words or phrases as *anger, unnecessary, fear, waste of time, people getting hurt, confusion, frustration,* and *low morale.*

3. After listing 8 to 12 words in the negative column on your flipchart, ask participants to share some of the words or phrases they listed under the positive column. You are likely to hear such words or phrases as *opportunity, efficiencies, new ideas, better service, improvement, getting out of a rut,* and *excitement.*

4. When you have listed 8 to 12 words in the positive column, ask participants to offer their observations about the words in the two columns. Listen to a few comments and then ask participants to identify what, from their perspectives, makes the difference as to whether a person perceives a change as positive or negative.

5. Participants are likely to offer such responses as past experience with the person or group initiating the change, how well people felt the organization dealt with them during previous changes, whether someone sees a change as positive or negative in its effects on them, how much order and structure an individual needs to feel comfortable, and whether someone feels that they can direct or influence change or whether the change was beyond their influence or control.

DEBRIEFING

Once participants have offered their comments on the factors that influence which perception of change someone develops, make the following integrating comments and suggestions:

1. The response people have to change results both from actions that an organization or its change leaders take and the very personal way that individuals view a change (for example, as a threat that will take away something that they value or as an opportunity).

2. Helping ourselves and others through the change process, then, involves looking both within ourselves and to those within the organization who are causing a given change.

3. Suggest that much of an individual's response to change is a function of how much control or influence he or she has over the change. Offer the metaphor that the difference between viewing a change as either negative or positive can be compared to taking a car trip. We could be seated next to the driver with a hand on the steering wheel or we can be totally cut off from the driver—locked in the trunk, blindfolded, with our mouths taped shut. Our location and hence our ability to participate in planning the trip would have a great effect on our perception of it as positive or negative. Suggest that it is likewise evident, from the comments offered by the participants, that our level of control or influence over a change plays an important part in how we view it.

4. Conclude by noting that although people have a choice in how they respond to change, staying in the "negative" column has consequences for their health and well-being. People who stay on the negative side eventually get sick—physically or emotionally or both. When people shift their focus toward seeing the positives of change, they begin to move out of "dis-ease" and into an active, healthy response.

Training Instrument 9–1
Perceptions of Change

Instructions: What are your negative and positive perceptions of the changes you have experienced or observed? Develop two lists of words or phrases that describe the negative and positive perceptions you have about change in your life or work.

NEGATIVE PERCEPTIONS	POSITIVE PERCEPTIONS

Learning Activity 9–2: Experiencing Personal Change

OBJECTIVES

The objectives of this learning activity are to enable participants to

- realize the nature of their own emotional journeys through the change process

- see that the journey people experience during change is natural and inevitable

- accept responsibility for their own mental health throughout the change process

- identify actions that both individuals affected by a change and those who are initiating the change can take to reduce its negative effects and increase commitment to the change.

MATERIALS

The materials needed for this activity are

- Training Instrument 9–2: Experiencing Personal Change

- Training Instrument 9–3: Characteristics of and Actions for Each Phase of the Change Journey

- Handout 9–1: The Journey through Change

- Flipchart and marking pens

- PowerPoint slides 7–6 through 7–12.

TIME

- 50 minutes

PREPARATIONS

Prior to this learning activity, ensure that each participant has a copy of the handout and have a blank flipchart page and markers ready.

INSTRUCTIONS

1. Distribute Training Instrument 9–2. Ask participants to turn to the instrument and think of a change they recently have personally experienced. Indicate that this change should be one that is entirely behind them rather than one that may still be happening. Suggest that the change they think about could be a change in their personal lives (such as getting married, getting divorced, taking a new job, becoming the chair of a community group, or moving to a new house) or in their current or past jobs.

2. Indicate that the change that they think of can be perceived by them as either positive or negative or as a change that they initiated or that was initiated by others.

3. Ask them to take 30 seconds to think about this change and then to write a brief description of the change on which they will focus as you lead them into the next step of the activity.

4. After 30 seconds, recapture the group's attention. Suggest that you'd like them to imagine that, during the change they have just identified, they had kept a personal journal where they recorded their thoughts, feelings, and reactions at different times throughout the change process.

5. Display the first question on PowerPoint slide 7–6. Ask participants to open their "journals" to the "preamble"—written in the days and weeks before they knew the change was upon them—and to jot down the words or phrases that they see in the journal that described their thoughts, feelings, and reactions before they knew change was happening. Give participants about 45 seconds to write their responses in the space next to the "1." on Training Instrument 9–2.

6. Proceed through the next three points on the PowerPoint slide using the same process as in step 5:

  ◆ Ask them to turn to the first few pages of their journal. In the earliest days of the change, what were the thoughts, reactions, and feelings they had recorded on these initial pages of their journals? Have them place their responses to the right of the "2."

  ◆ Ask them to turn to the midpoint of their journals (just past the staples!) and to record the thoughts, reactions, and feelings they see written the middle of their journals. Have them place their responses to the right of the "3."

♦ Finally, reveal the last question on the PowerPoint slide. Ask them to turn to the last page of their "mind's-eye" change journal and to record the words they see written just before the words "The End." Have them place their responses to the right of the "4."

7. Recapture the attention of the group. Indicate that for the next 10 minutes they will team up with others at their table to explore the areas of common ground and differences in how each experienced a recent change.

8. Display PowerPoint slide 7–7 and direct the groups to discuss

♦ the reactions, thoughts, and feelings that they have in common as a group for each of the four journal entries

♦ whether being "locked in the trunk" or having a "hand on the wheel" from the passenger's seat during the "roadtrip" made a difference in how the trip was perceived

♦ whether perceiving the change as either negative or positive made a difference

♦ whether the change occurring in their personal or professional lives made a difference.

9. Ask each group to select a leader to guide their group discussion. Give the groups 8 to 10 minutes to talk through the four journal entries and to respond to the discussion questions from the slide.

10. After 8 to 10 minutes, reconvene the large group and, using a round-robin approach, record examples of the words describing what people experienced in response to the four journal questions. (*Note:* Begin with a blank flipchart page, but imagine that the page is divided equally into four quarters. Start writing words in response to the first question in the upper left corner. Continue listing words in this quarter of the flipchart page, making sure not to go beyond the imaginary lines on the flipchart that divide the page into quarters. Move quickly and don't discuss the words, except to clarify if necessary.)

11. Move to the second question. Begin recording the words offered by the groups at the top of the lower left quadrant of the flipchart page. For the third question, record the words at the top of the lower right flipchart page quadrant. And, for the last question, record the words at the top of the upper right quadrant. The words or phrases that you are likely to hear for each question are listed in table 9–1.

Table 9–1
Likely Responses to Four Journal Questions

COMFORT AND CONTROL	LEARNING, ACCEPTANCE, AND COMMITMENT
Comfortable	Now I know
Safe	Energized
Everything's fine	Success!
Happy	We made it!
Satisfied	Relief
No problems	Wow!
Positive	Self-confidence
Rewarding	Satisfied
I'm okay, you're okay!	Comfortable
	What's next?

FEAR, ANGER, AND RESISTANCE	INQUIRY, EXPERIMENTATION, AND DISCOVERY
Frustration	Confused
Anger	Questioning
Fearful	Hopeful
Betrayed	Opportunity
Upset	Frustrated
Confused	Disappointed
Hostility	Challenged
Anxiety	Half-way there!
Self-doubt	Making progress
Lost	Going in all directions at once!
Dazed	Searching for solutions
Challenged	Exciting
	Innovation/creativity

12. Once all four flipchart quadrants have been completed, point out to the group that they have just described the emotional journey—sometimes long and difficult—that people often experience throughout the change process. Display PowerPoint slide 7–8. Reveal each of the four phases of the journey and suggest that this journey is natural and inevitable and that understanding how this process works is the key to not only helping themselves through any change but also helping others through it.

13. Distribute Handout 9–1 and Training Instrument 9–3. Walk the large group through the four phases of the emotional journey of change. Draw lines on the flipchart marking the four quadrants and write the name of each quadrant on the flipchart page as you discuss the characteristics of each phase.

14. For each phase you discuss, highlight the words offered by the group and note that many of these reactions have been listed by past workshop participants. Indicate that, in some cases, people offer words that seem out of place. (You can cite an example of someone in the Comfort and Control phase of change feeling uneasy and uncomfortable.) Ask the group why this might be. Respond that, especially at the ending of a phase, people may begin to experience a transition in their feelings and reactions that hint at the next phase—even though they may not have yet entered that new phase.

15. As you discuss each phase of the change journey, display the appropriate PowerPoint slide listing common characteristics of each phase (PowerPoint slides 7–9 through 7–12) and ask participants to make notes on the left-hand column on Training Instrument 9–3 to reflect characteristics of each phase.

16. Note that at some point in the Fear, Anger, and Resistance phase, people make a choice (conscious or unconscious) to shift their attention away from looking backward and begin looking forward. Suggest that, at this point, the individual has reconciled himself or herself to the inevitability of the change and has decided to make it work.

17. Once you have walked the group through the four phases of the emotional journey of change, offer some additional comments to help people understand the model:

   ◆ People can move in either direction around the circle. Those in Fear, Anger, and Resistance can, for example, try to ignore the pressure for change and simply slide back into Comfort and Control. The frustrations that people sometimes feel in Inquiry, Experimentation, and Discovery can cause some to flee back into resisting the change.

◆ Note the two dimensions: looking back versus looking forward and stability versus chaos. Suggest that stable environments create conditions that support Comfort and Control—and that being comfortable and in control involve holding on to what we have (looking back). Indicate that as change is introduced, the stable environment begins to descend into instability or even chaos. The fear, anger, and resistance people often feel as stability gradually disappears and instability emerges results from the loss of the comfort and control that people experienced in the past (looking back). At the highest point of instability and chaos, those people who don't flee back to Comfort and Control (and a state of denial) or stand and fight the change begin to abandon any hope of salvation from the past and, with varying degrees of enthusiasm, begin looking forward by making efforts to create a new stability and make the change work for them.

◆ People can spend three days at any one phase or can get "stuck" and spend 30 years there.

◆ Remind participants of the point made earlier in the debriefing of Learning Activity 9–1: Getting stuck in fear, anger, and resistance can take its toll on personal health and job performance. Feeling victimized by the change and the organization can lead to a negative energy that ends up attacking one's stomach lining as much as it tries to fight the change.

◆ The challenge in the Learning, Acceptance, and Commitment phase is that people may shift their focus away from being open to new opportunities and changes and instead try to hold on to what they have achieved (focusing on past successes). This may lead to a gradual drift into Comfort and Control—and the cycle begins again.

◆ Members of a team may be in different phases at the same time. People move through change in different ways: Some hang onto Comfort and Control, others continue to fight the change by staying in the Fear, Anger, and Resistance phase. Still others are already committed and preparing for the next change.

18. Ask the large group to offer their comments on whether there was a difference in how people responded to change based on the degree of influence or control they had over the change (locked in the car's trunk or having a hand on the wheel), whether they perceived the change as negative or positive, and whether the change was personal or professional. Draw answers from the groups and summarize by suggesting that even a positive change that we initiate ourselves (such as getting married) brings out some level of instability and chaos and, hence, fear and resistance. Indicate that an important distinction of change that we view as positive or over which we have control is that we are likely to spend less time looking backward (in the Comfort and Control and Fear, Anger, and Resistance phases). Our journey through the Inquiry, Experimentation, and Discovery phase is also likely to be less frustrating as we work to find answers to the questions posed by the change.

DEBRIEFING

Complete this activity by suggesting to participants that understanding why people respond to change the way they do is the key to helping them through the change. Once we understand how change affects us emotionally and why we take the actions we do when faced with change, we are much more able to help ourselves (and others) through change.

Indicate that the next learning activity explores actions that individuals can take to guide themselves and others through the emotional journey of change.

Training Instrument 9–2

Experiencing Personal Change

Instructions: Consider a change (personal or professional) that you have experienced from *start to finish* in the recent past. Imagine that you kept a journal throughout the change process—a place where you jotted down your *feelings, reactions,* and *thoughts* at different times during the change.

The change I am thinking of is _____

_____

_____

Now imagine that you have opened your change journal to read what you had written on specific pages . . .

 1.

 2.

 3.

 4.

Training Instrument 9-3

Characteristics of and Actions for Each Phase of the Change Journey

Instructions: Consider the characteristics of each of the four phases of change, listed below in the left-hand column. Then describe, in the right-hand column, actions that you can take to help yourself and others through each phase.

CHARACTERISTICS OF EACH CHANGE PHASE	ACTIONS PEOPLE CAN TAKE TO HELP THEMSELVES (A) AND OTHERS (B) THROUGH THIS PHASE OF CHANGE
Comfort and Control:	(a) Self:
◆ Comfortable	
◆ Safe	
◆ Everything's fine	
◆ Happy	
◆ Satisfied	(b) Others:
◆ No problems	
◆ Positive	
◆ Rewarding	
◆ In control . . .	
◆ I'm okay, you're okay!	
Fear, Anger, and Resistance:	(a) Self:
◆ Frustration	
◆ Anger	
◆ Fearful	
◆ Betrayed	
◆ Upset	(b) Others:
◆ Confused	
◆ Challenged	
◆ Hostility	
◆ Anxiety	
◆ Self-doubt	
◆ Lost	
◆ Dazed	

continued on next page

Training Instrument 9–3, continued

Characteristics of and Actions for Each Phase of the Change Journey

Inquiry, Experimentation, and Discovery:

(a) Self:

- Confused
- Questioning
- Hopeful
- Opportunity
- Frustrated
- Disappointed
- Challenged
- Half-way there!
- Making progress
- Exciting!
- Searching for solutions
- Going in all directions at once!
- Innovation/creativity

(b) Others:

Learning, Acceptance, and Commitment:

(a) Self:

- Now I know!
- Energized
- Success!
- We made it!
- Relief
- Wow!
- Self-confidence
- Satisfied
- Comfortable
- What's next?

(b) Others:

Handout 9-1
The Journey through Change

When people encounter a change at work or in their personal lives, whether they perceive it as positive or negative, their response tends to follow a natural and predictable pattern.

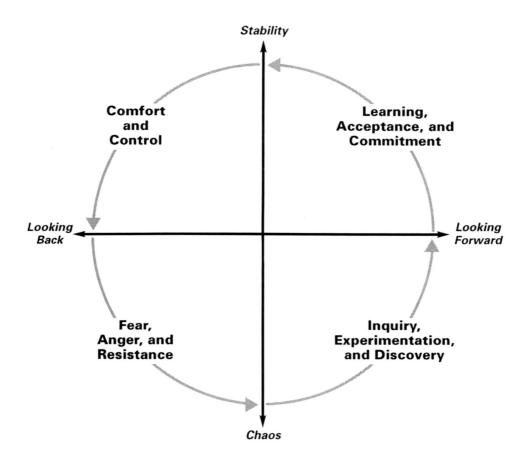

Learning Activity 9–3:
Guiding People through the Change Journey

OBJECTIVES

The objectives of this learning activity are to

- identify specific actions that participants can take to enable them to develop a healthy response to a change they are experiencing (how to take care of themselves)

- identify specific actions that participants—especially managers and supervisors—can take to help others through the change process.

MATERIALS

The materials needed for this activity are

- Training Instrument 9–3: Characteristics of and Actions for Each Phase of the Change Journey

- Training Instrument 9–4: Personal Plan for Helping Yourself and Others through Change

- Handout 9–2: Actions for Guiding People through Change

- PowerPoint slides 7–13 through 7–18.

TIME

- 50 minutes

PREPARATIONS

- This activity immediately follows Learning Activity 9–2 and uses the same change model and one of the instruments introduced in Learning Activity 9–2.

INSTRUCTIONS

1. Ask participants as a large group to consider the long-term emotional and physical consequences for (or toll on) the individual if he or she gets stuck at any phase in this journey—especially in the first

three phases. Referring to the flipchart page you completed with the group in Learning Activity 9–2, invite comments and responses to the question on the consequences of getting stuck in a phase.

2. As people respond to each phase, display PowerPoint slide 7–13, reinforcing what people have offered as consequences. Suggest that the personal consequence for getting stuck in each phase can be significant: in the Comfort and Control phase, complacency and obsolescence; in the Fear, Anger, and Resistance phase, sickness and depression; and in the Inquiry, Experimentation, and Discovery phase, anxiety and lack of integration—where the change ideas never "gel" and the person never quite feels connected to the change.

3. Note that the challenge in the Learning, Acceptance, and Commitment phase is sustaining the change and preparing people for the next one. Getting stuck in the Learning, Acceptance, and Commitment phase is, in the short run, a good thing. Over the long term, however, the desire to sustain commitment to the new way of doing business may prevent people from considering even better alternatives or further changes. This becomes a problem if people become complacent with the new order and strive to hang on to what has been achieved rather than to embrace new learning. This desire to hang on to what has been attained can lead people back into the Comfort and Control phase.

4. Suggest to participants that although understanding how people respond emotionally during a change is fundamental to effectively helping them deal with these reactions, moving people into the next phase is critical for their own health and to enable progress. Indicate that avoiding getting stuck involves taking actions to address their questions, fears, anxieties, and doubts.

5. Note that this learning activity explores actions that both individuals affected by the change and those who are driving or leading the change can take to help themselves and others get unstuck and continue their emotional journey through the change process.

6. Refer to Training Instrument 9–3. Point out that they have already identified what people are experiencing at each phase of the change process. Indicate that over the next half-hour the group will complete the right-hand column by exploring the things they can do during a change for themselves and the things they can do for oth-

ers. Suggest that this second focus (doing for others) is especially important for those who are in supervisory and managerial positions and for those who are leading the change in the organization.

7. Assign each of the four phases of the change journey to a small group of participants. If you have more than four groups in your session, you will need to assign one or more phases to more than one group. Ask each group to select a discussion leader and, displaying PowerPoint slide 7–14, ask each group to develop two lists in the space provided on the appropriate section of Training Instrument 9–3: first, actions that people can take to help themselves and, second, actions that they can take to help others through their respective phase of the change journey. (*Note:* Ask the group assigned to the Learning, Acceptance, and Commitment phase to focus on actions to sustain that phase and avoid slipping back into the Comfort and Control phase.) Indicate that each group will be asked to report on their action strategies for their assigned phase. Give the groups five to eight minutes for this activity.

8. After five to eight minutes, call the large group back together and begin leading a discussion of appropriate actions for each phase of the emotional journey through change.

9. As each group reports its recommendations for actions to help themselves and others, encourage other participants to take notes in the appropriate section of Training Instrument 9–3. Indicate that you will be sharing your own list of possible actions.

10. As each group completes its report, summarize and reinforce what they have offered and then display the appropriate PowerPoint slide (7–15 through 7–18) offering your ideas for action and noting that you have an additional handout that includes these ideas.

11. Distribute Handout 9–2 (Actions for Guiding People through Change).

DEBRIEFING

After the small groups of participants have offered their ideas for helping themselves and others through change and you have shared PowerPoint slides 7–15 through 7–18 and Handout 9–2, make the following integrating comments:

1. The emotional journey through change is both natural and inevitable, but people and organizations can get stuck in any phase and subsequently experience significant negative effects.

2. Individuals can prevent some of the negative effects the participants have discussed by taking responsibility for shaping the change, for improving the change, and for exploring solutions that meet both their needs and the needs of the organization.

3. As time permits, refer to William Bridges' work on the transitions of change (see the Further Reading section), noting that according to his research, the change process begins with the "endings" of what has been and the grief about the loss that often ensues. It then moves through a confusing period that he calls the "neutral zone," in which people are pulled both ahead into the future and back into the past, with the final transition being "new beginnings"—a period filled with all the opportunity and optimism of a fresh start.

4. Note that it is also important that we make an effort to help others through the change process. Indicate that this responsibility is especially important for those in supervisory or managerial positions.

5. Direct participants to Training Instrument 9–4: Personal Plan for Helping Yourself and Others through Change. Ask them to spend the next five minutes identifying some specific actions and steps that they will take to help both themselves and others through the change process.

6. As time permits, ask each participant to pair up with another person at the table to share their personal plans. Encourage the pairs to help each other strengthen their personal plans by offering additional strategies and ideas for helping themselves and others through the change.

Training Instrument 9–4

Personal Plan for Helping Yourself and Others through Change

Instructions: Reflect on where you and most of your team are located in the Journey through Change Model and check that phase below:

☐ Comfort and Control   ☐ Learning, Acceptance, and Commitment

☐ Fear, Anger, and Resistance   ☐ Inquiry, Experimentation, and Discovery

Identify the specific actions that you can take to help yourself and others move into the next phase of the change journey and toward learning and commitment. If your team is already in learning and commitment, what actions can you take to sustain continuous learning and commitment?

Actions to Help Yourself:

Actions to Help Others:

1.

2.

3.

4.

5.

6.

Handout 9–2

Actions for Guiding People through Change

Comfort and Control

- Acknowledge their successful past.
- Get people's attention! Give people a reason to pay attention so they hear the need for change.
- Sell the need for change . . . sell the pain and the consequences of *not* changing.
- Immerse people in specific information about the change . . . customer complaints, budget data, increasing costs, competitive pressures.
- Let people know it will happen—one way or another!
- Give people time to let the ideas sink in.
- Don't sell the solutions . . . sell the problem.

Fear, Anger, and Resistance

- Co-create the vision—involve others in defining the future.
- Listen, listen, listen.
- Acknowledge people's pain, perceived losses, and anger.
- Strive to address their perceived losses by adjusting the change vision and strategy.
- Tell people what you know—and what you don't know.
- Don't try to talk people out of their feelings.
- Discuss ways to *solve* the problems people see with the change.
- Encourage discussion, dissent, disagreement, debate . . . keep people talking.

Learning, Acceptance, and Commitment

- Acknowledge their hard work.
- Celebrate successes and accomplishments.
- Reaffirm the vision.
- Bring people together toward the vision.
- Acknowledge what people have left behind.
- Develop long-term goals and plans.
- Provide tools and training to reinforce new behaviors.
- Reinforce and reward the new behaviors.
- Create systems or structures that reinforce new behaviors.
- Prepare people for the next change.

Inquiry, Experimentation, and Discovery

- Give people as much freedom *and* direction as you can.
- Give people permission to find their own solutions.
- Encourage people to take risks.
- Affirm and refine the vision—make room for others' ideas.
- Tell people as much as you know.
- Encourage teamwork/collaboration.
- Encourage personal reflection and learning.
- Provide people training and support.
- Set short-term goals.

Learning Activity 9–4:
Introducing and Leading a Change

This activity, geared toward managers, supervisors, and change leaders, immediately follows Learning Activity 9–3.

OBJECTIVES

The objectives of this learning activity are to

- identify the step-by-step process for introducing change in an organization

- demonstrate the relationship between introducing a change and the emotional reactions exhibited by those affected by it.

MATERIALS

The materials needed for this activity are

- Training Instrument 9–5: Introducing, Leading, and Sustaining Commitment to a Change

- Training Instrument 9–6: Personal Plan for Initiating and Sustaining a Change

- Handout 9–3: An Integrated Model for Leading Change

- Handout 9–4: Actions for Introducing and Leading Change

- Flipchart and marking pens if desired

- PowerPoint slides 7–19 through 7–24.

TIME

- 50 minutes

INSTRUCTIONS

1. Suggest to participants that so far this program has explored the emotional impact of change on those who are affected by it and we have discussed the actions that leaders can take to ease people through the transitions of change and move toward change commitment. Indicate that there is another set of actions leaders must consider—the actual steps they must take to introduce change.

2. Distribute Handout 9–3 and display PowerPoint slide 7–19. Indicate that this integrated change leadership model both includes the four phases of the journey through change that have been recently explored and adds a new layer: the actions that leaders, managers, and supervisors must take to introduce and sustain a change initiative. Emphasize the point that the "goodness" of a change idea or initiative doesn't guarantee that others will embrace it. Building employee commitment involves not only responding to the affective responses to the change initiative but also developing a carefully planned approach for introducing the new ideas, methods, and strategies to the organization.

3. Using PowerPoint slide 7–19, give a brief overview of the four stages for introducing and sustaining change. Suggest that, at each stage, leaders must engage in specific activities that introduce the new ideas, manage the emotional responses of those affected by the change, address key challenges, and sustain ongoing commitment to the change. (As time allows, you may want to refer to Kurt Lewin's three-stage change model [Lewin, 1951], noting the parallels with this integrated change leadership model [Handout 9–3]: the first stage involves unfreezing the status quo [creating a felt need]; the second, introducing the change ideas; and, third, refreezing [stabilizing and reinforcing]. You may want to sketch Lewin's three-stage process on a flipchart to help emphasize the parallels between the two models.)

4. Distribute Training Instrument 9–5. Display PowerPoint slide 7–20. Explain that, for the next activity, you'd like them to think of a specific change that their organization is implementing, either now or in the near future. With this change in mind, ask them to identify specific actions that leaders should take for each stage of the change leadership process. Assign one stage of the process to each small group. Give each small group eight minutes to identify at least three actions they would recommend to change leaders.

5. After approximately eight minutes, reconvene the large group and ask each small group to report its recommendations for leadership action. Record on flipchart pages if desired and time permits. Following the groups' reports on each stage, display the appropriate PowerPoint slide (7–21 through 7–24) with additional suggestions for action. As you present the slides, note that these suggested actions are generic strategies that leaders should take for nearly all

change initiatives. Distribute Handout 9–4, which summarizes the actions for leaders at each stage of initiating a change.

DEBRIEFING

Once the small groups have suggested actions for managers, supervisors, and change leaders for each step of the change process and you have shared Handout 9–4, make the following summary comments:

1. Those who lead change have a dual role: introducing the change and responding to the emotional fallout from its introduction. Understanding the importance of fulfilling both roles is essential for a successful change initiative.

2. The success of a change initiative is far from certain. Thoughtful leaders must bring a deep understanding of the process for both introducing a new idea and for helping people through the transition from a place of comfort (where they feel in control) through anger, fear, confusion, and anxiety to a place where they develop commitment to the change.

3. It is only by effectively managing these parallel worlds—pushing and facilitating—that the change leader is likely to experience success.

4. There are no guarantees that doing everything right will lead to a successful change initiative, but doing the right things in the right way will significantly increase the likelihood of success.

5. Emphasize that the leader's actions for introducing and sustaining a change represent some of the key elements of a plan for implementing change. Encourage those who are leading a change initiative to use the ideas generated during this discussion on the actions for change leadership as the beginning steps for developing a formal strategy for implementing the change.

6. Direct participants to Training Instrument 9–6: Personal Plan for Initiating Change. Ask them to spend the next five minutes identifying some specific actions and steps they will take to initiate and build commitment to a given change in their area.

7. As time permits, ask each participant to pair up with another person at the table to share their personal plans. Encourage the pairs to help each other strengthen their personal plans by offering additional strategies and ideas for initiating and sustaining change.

Training Instrument 9–5

Introducing, Leading, and Sustaining Commitment to a Change

Instructions: Reflect on a specific change that your organization is implementing now or in the near future. Identify the specific actions that you and other change leaders can take to initiate the change, respond to the respective phase of the emotional journey, and meet the key challenge of each phase.

STAGE OF INTRODUCING AND LEADING CHANGE	ACTIONS LEADERS CAN TAKE TO INITIATE AND SUSTAIN CHANGE IN THIS ORGANIZATION
Create a Felt Need ◆ *Phase of the Emotional Journey:* Comfort and Control ◆ *Key Challenge:* Moving people out of their comfortable complacency	
Introduce the New Ideas ◆ *Phase of the Emotional Journey:* Anger, Fear, and Resistance ◆ *Key Challenge:* Dealing with anger, fear, and resistance while inviting involvement in creating a shared vision of the change	
Revise and Finalize the Change Plan ◆ *Phase of the Emotional Journey:* Inquiry, Experimentation, and Discovery ◆ *Key Challenge:* Helping people deal with the anxiety and confusion, answering their questions, and integrating their ideas into the change plan	
Stabilize and Sustain the Change ◆ *Phase of the Emotional Journey:* Learning, Acceptance, and Commitment ◆ *Key Challenge:* Sustaining ongoing commitment to the change while increasing readiness for the next change	

Training Instrument 9–6
Personal Plan for Initiating and Sustaining a Change

Instructions: Reflect on the inner circle of the Integrated Model for Leading Change (Handout 9–3) and the actions that change leaders should take to initiate and sustain an organizational change.

Based on the Integrated Model for Leading Change and the emotional responses people are demonstrating as the change is introduced, identify the actions that you can take at *each step* of the process to more effectively introduce and sustain change. Refer to your Personal Plan for Helping Yourself and Others through Change (Training Instrument 9–4) for additional ideas on actions you can take to successfully initiate and sustain the change.

Create a Felt Need:

Introduce the Change:

Revise and Finalize the Change Plan:

Stabilize and Sustain the Change:

Handout 9–3
An Integrated Model for Leading Change

People begin their emotional journey through a change (the outer circle) in response to the actions that leaders and others take in introducing a change (the inner circle). Further, the actions leaders take when initiating a change must also respond to the needs, questions, issues, and emotional reactions that people experience as they move along their journeys through change.

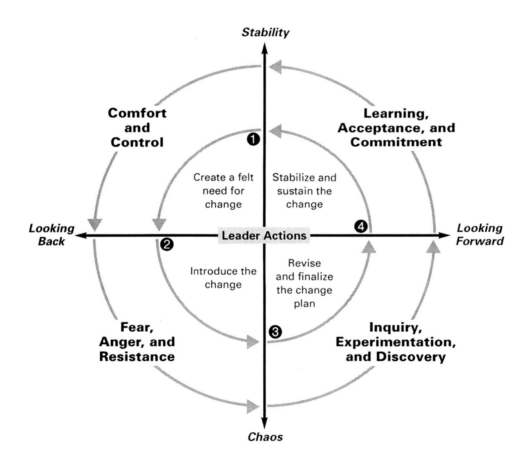

Handout 9–4

Actions for Introducing and Leading Change

At each stage of the process for introducing and leading change the change leader must understand where those affected by the change are in their emotional journeys and then take an active role in leading people out of their current phases and into the next stage of their journeys.

At each emotional phase of the journey, there is a key challenge that the change leader must address.

Create a Felt Need—*Key Challenge:* Moving people out of comfortable complacency and into a readiness for change

- Identify what needs to change.
- Identify *why* it must change; identify the problem that needs to be solved.
- Immerse them in the data from the customer, from other stakeholders, from the organization's performance successes or failures.
- Identify the *consequences* for the organization of not solving the problem or not responding to the challenge.
- Get their attention; give people a reason to move out of comfort and complacency.

Introduce the New Ideas—*Key Challenge:* Dealing with anger, fear, and resistance while inviting involvement in creating a shared vision of the change

- Ask people to explore ideas that help solve the "problem" that people now realize must be solved.
- Offer possible solutions and strategies that address the challenge/problem.
- Work together with others to co-create a vision of the change—ensure that it is a shared vision.
- Guide people in exploring the positive outcomes of the change; help them see the benefits and opportunities that the change presents.
- Listen to people's objections, concerns, fears, and perceived losses.
- Acknowledge their fears and what they perceive they may lose.
- Invite people to offer their own solutions to offset the perceived losses and strategies to realize the benefits; suggest your own ideas of possible gains and opportunities.
- Integrate their concerns about the change and their ideas for improving it into strategies that address their concerns.

Revise and Finalize the Change Plan—*Key Challenge:* Helping people deal with the anxiety and confusion, answering their questions, and integrating their ideas into the change plan

- Help people to (a) identify and explore the hidden opportunities, (b) define the future of the change on their terms and those of the organization, and (c) invent creative solutions to the challenges facing them and the organization.

continued on next page

Handout 9–4, continued

Actions for Introducing and Leading Change

- ◆ Continue to identify obstacles to change acceptance that must be overcome and explore the hidden opportunities that emerge when overcoming each obstacle.
- ◆ Encourage people to find creative answers to their questions about the change and their future role after the change is complete.
- ◆ Adjust the change vision, strategy, and plan in response to the ideas and answers offered by stakeholders.

Stabilize and Sustain the Change—*Key Challenge:* Sustaining ongoing commitment to the change while increasing readiness for the next change

- ◆ Identify and develop action steps for stabilizing, reinforcing, and sustaining the change. These might include giving people time to mourn their actual losses, providing skill and knowledge training, revising job descriptions, developing new reward systems, strengthening social connections and relationships, and recognizing and celebrating accomplishments.
- ◆ Develop performance measures to evaluate the results from the change.
- ◆ Make adjustments to the change vision and strategy to reflect new learning and insights.
- ◆ Challenge people to be open to new challenges, forces, and pressures for the next change.
- ◆ Key questions to explore:
  - ◆ How will the losses that have actually been experienced be mourned? How will the gains people have made be recognized and celebrated?
  - ◆ What skills, knowledge, and attitudes need to be developed in people to sustain their commitment to the new ways of thinking and acting?
  - ◆ Where will people find stability, focus, and clarity during the change?
  - ◆ What organizational systems and infrastructures are needed to support and reinforce the new directions, ways of thinking, behaviors, and so forth?
  - ◆ How will the new ideas, roles, expectations, goals, behaviors, and methods be preserved and integrated into new standard practices?
  - ◆ How will continuous learning and improvement be sustained?
  - ◆ How will people be encouraged to continue challenging the status quo—even the new status quo?
  - ◆ How can the organization slow the drift into the complacency of comfort and control?
  - ◆ What are the signs of emerging complacency? How will the organization respond?

Learning Activity 9–5:
The Forces Causing Change

OBJECTIVES

The purpose of this activity is either to help change leaders create a sense of urgency (a felt need for change) among those to be affected by a change or to help those affected by the change to understand the need to change on their own.

The objectives of this learning activity are to

- identify the broad forces causing change in society and organizations today

- identify the specific forces causing change in the participants' organization.

MATERIALS

The materials needed for this activity are

- Training Instrument 9–7: The Forces Driving Change

- Training Instrument 9–8: Responding to the Forces for Change

- Flipchart and marking pens

- PowerPoint slides 7–25 through 7–29.

TIME

- 45 minutes

PREPARATIONS

This activity can be geared to managers, supervisors, leaders of change, or those affected by the change. How the activity is introduced and facilitated depends, to a degree, upon the audience. Typically, this activity would follow Learning Activity 9–4.

INSTRUCTIONS

1. Display PowerPoint slide 7–25. Ask participants to describe the point the British mathematician and philosopher Alfred North Whitehead was making about the nature of change. Summarize participant re-

actions by suggesting that progress results from the balance of forces: stability and order on one side and change and instability on the other. Note that the extreme of each has its own set of negative consequences for the organization (from obsolescence for stability and order to disintegration for change and instability).

2. Point out that the value of change is that it introduces pressure on people in the organization that may, in turn, cause them to think, decide, and act in a new way. If their thinking is informed by a clear understanding of these environmental and internal forces for change, then the change enables the organization to remain healthy, vital, and effective over the long term.

3. State that initiating organizational change just for the sake of change serves no productive purpose. Emphasize that every useful change is caused by forces both inside and outside of the organization. Any thoughtful change that leaders may initiate, then, must be anchored to these forces. The desired change should be designed to help sustain the organization's long-term relevance and effectiveness by anticipating and preparing for the effects of these forces.

4. Distribute Training Instrument 9–7 and display PowerPoint slide 7–26.

5. Guide participants through each of the external forces that commonly cause change. Give current examples of each external force.

6. Suggest that, as the handout indicates, the forces for change can just as easily come from within the organization—often at the same time as those from outside.

7. Briefly guide participants through each of the internal forces that commonly cause change from within organizations (see chapter 2 of this workbook). Give contemporary examples of each force. Point out that often the internal forces evolve from the external forces (for example, performance failures from changes in the economy or market niche) or that the internal force may reinforce what exists as an external force (for example, leadership and vision involving technology or human or social needs and values).

8. State that in order to better understand the reasons behind the changes that may be needed in their own organization it is critical to identify the specific internal and external forces that are putting pressure on the organization.

9. Display PowerPoint slide 7–27. Ask participants to work in small groups to identify the most significant forces (either external or internal) that are driving change in their organization. Also ask them to identify the consequences for the organization if it doesn't effectively respond to these changes. Give participants approximately eight minutes for this activity.

10. After about eight minutes, reconvene the large group and ask each of the small groups to share its responses to the first question (the most significant and powerful forces that are causing the change in the organization). Record these forces on a flipchart as time permits.

11. Once the list of key forces is developed, ask the large group to offer ideas about which of these important forces is most significant to the future success of the organization.

12. Invite participants to share what they identified as the consequences for the organization if it doesn't find an effective response to this current or future force for change.

13. Suggest that "creating a felt need" is the first step in introducing any organizational change and that, by understanding the consequences of not preparing for and responding to the forces for change, those who are leading a change are likely to find more success at initiating and sustaining a change. Also, those who are affected by a change are more likely to accept the need for the change.

14. Select the top two or three forces for change. Display PowerPoint slide 7–28 and distribute Training Instrument 9–8. Ask each small group to identify at least three constructive ways in which the organization can effectively respond to this force for change. Encourage them to think about positive ways that the organization can both respond to this force for change and respond to employee needs during the change. Give the groups about seven minutes for this.

15. Facilitate a discussion of participant ideas for responding to the forces for change. If desired, record these ideas on flipchart paper and save for reference following the workshop.

DEBRIEFING

1. Display PowerPoint slide 7–29. Note that "change is inevitable, growth is optional" and that better understanding the forces that are

likely to influence the organization's future success is an important first step in getting people to accept the need for change (growth).

2. Highlight the importance of involving the people who will be affected by the forces for change in exploring both the consequences of not responding and their ideas for how the organization should respond.

3. Point out that, although helping people see the need for change makes it easier to develop acceptance of a given change, acceptance involves much more than simply acknowledging that a change is necessary. The next critical step in helping people through change involves understanding what people might lose as they move from a place of comfort and control to one filled with uncertainty and doubt.

Training Instrument 9–7

The Forces Driving Change

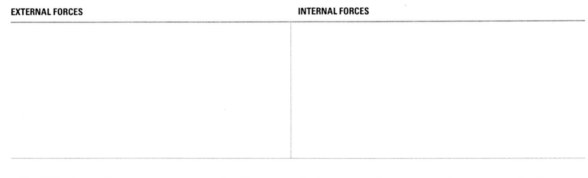

> **External Forces**
> Technology
> Economy
> Market Niche
> Human/Social Needs & Values
> Government Policies

> **Internal Forces**
> Leadership & Vision
> Performance Failures
> Workforce Demographics
> Employee Dissatisfaction
> New Ideas

1. What are the external and internal forces driving change in this organization? Make a list of the external and internal forces that are putting pressure on the organization to be other than what it has been or is now.

EXTERNAL FORCES	INTERNAL FORCES

2. What are the consequences for the organization, employees, customers, and other stakeholders if the organization doesn't effectively respond to these forces for change?

THE CONSEQUENCES IF WE DON'T EFFECTIVELY RESPOND TO THESE FORCES   6

Training Instrument 9–8

Responding to the Forces for Change

Instructions: Based on our discussion of the most significant forces (external or internal) driving change in this organization, identify at least three constructive ways in which the organization (its leaders and staff) can effectively respond to this force for change.

KEY FORCES DRIVING CHANGE IN THIS ORGANIZATION	AT LEAST THREE CONSTRUCTIVE ACTIONS THAT THE ORGANIZATION'S LEADERS AND STAFF CAN TAKE

Learning Activity 9-6:
The Sources of Change Resistance

OBJECTIVES

The objectives of this learning activity are to

- identify why people tend to resist change

- have participants develop a plan for dealing with employees' and other stakeholders' resistance to change.

MATERIALS

The materials needed for this activity are

- Training Instrument 9–9: The Origins of Change Resistance

- Training Instrument 9–10: Personal Plan for Dealing with Change Resistance

- Handout 9–5: Why We Value Change Resisters

- Flipchart and marking pens

- PowerPoint slides 7–30 through 7–33.

TIME

- 35 minutes

PREPARATIONS

This activity, which is geared toward managers, supervisors, and change leaders, can be used at different times during a leading change workshop. As proposed in this book and outlined in chapter 7, however, this activity follows Learning Activity 9–5.

- If desired, prepare a blank flipchart page with the heading "People Resist Change Because . . ."

- If desired, prepare a blank flipchart page with two columns, one headed "Causes of Resistance" and the other "Actions to Reduce Resistance."

INSTRUCTIONS

1. Ask participants if people resist change. Almost to a person, they will say "yes." Ask if change resistance is inevitable. Most participants again will say "yes."

2. Suggest that, as we discovered earlier (Learning Activity 9–2), there is some degree of resistance with almost every change initiative. Add that understanding the sources of resistance helps explain both its intensity and duration and enables change leaders to significantly reduce its impact.

3. Display PowerPoint slide 7–30. Indicate that Machiavelli made it compellingly clear that change creates resistance in those who perceive that they may lose something because of it and only tepid support from those who might be better off after the change. Indicate that change leaders have their work cut out for them.

4. Ask participants what causes resistance. If desired, record their responses on the prepared flipchart page.

5. Show PowerPoint slide 7–31 as you distribute Training Instrument 9–9. If this is the managers' workshop, ask participants to think of the change initiative that they are introducing as they read this handout on their own. If this is the employees' workshop, ask participants to think of the organizational changes they are now experiencing as they read this handout. Ask them to make a note, as they read, of the sources of resistance that are most likely to be behind employees' (or other stakeholders') resistance to the change. Give them about two minutes to read this handout.

6. After two minutes, display PowerPoint slide 7–32 and direct participants to work in small groups to, first, discuss which of the reasons for change resistance on Training Instrument 9–9 are the most likely reasons for change resistance in their organization or for this change and, second, identify at least two or three actions that change leaders and those affected by a change can take to help reduce or eliminate that source of resistance. Give the groups about eight minutes to share their perceptions of the sources of resistance and the actions to reduce resistance.

7. After about eight minutes, reconvene the large group and lead a discussion of the common sources of change resistance for the organi-

zation and the actions that participants have identified to reduce it. If desired, record the most significant sources of change resistance and ideas for reducing it on flipchart paper. Reinforce the responses offered and suggest additional actions and strategies as desired.

DEBRIEFING

Offer the following summary comments:

1. Failure to anticipate, understand, and respond to the origins of resistance to change is one of the most significant contributors to the failure of most change initiatives.

2. Effective leaders actively take steps to deal with resistance to change *before* it surfaces. Resistance does not surprise them. They expect it and build a strategy to reduce it into their plan for implementing change.

3. Finally, ask the group to answer the question "Why should we value those who resist change?" After hearing several responses, display PowerPoint 7–33, distribute Handout 9–5, and briefly review the importance of change resisters in improving the overall change initiative.

4. If this is a manager's workshop, direct participants to Training Instrument 9–10: Personal Plan for Dealing with Change Resistance. Ask them to spend the next three minutes identifying some specific actions they will take to reduce resistance to a change in those most affected by it.

5. As time permits, ask each participant to pair up with another person at the table to share their personal plans. Encourage the pairs to help each other strengthen their personal plans by offering additional strategies and ideas for responding to resistance.

Training Instrument 9–9
The Origins of Change Resistance

Why do people tend to resist change? Here are some of the common reasons why someone might be hesitant to embrace a new way of thinking and acting.

Instructions: For each likely cause behind change resistance noted below on the left, identify actions that leaders and staffers can take to reduce the reasons behind the cause. Write these in the blank column on the right.

1. They Fear Losing Something That They Value

* The greater the expected loss, the greater the resistance.

* People's fear is based on their *perception* of the situation—it doesn't matter whether their beliefs are accurate.

* Common fears are *perceived* loss of status, power, social opportunities, a comfortable status quo, territory, future rewards or opportunities, sense of direction, established relationships, and competence.

2. They Lack Trust in Leaders or Misunderstand Their Motives

* People may believe that a specific change was designed to take advantage of them.

* People may be concerned about the unknown details and implications of the change.

* People may fear that if they let an acceptable change occur now, it will set a precedent for allowing later changes with which they don't agree.

* People are likely to resist change when the political or civil service leadership is not trusted or respected.

continued on next page

Training Instrument 9–9, continued

The Origins of Change Resistance

---

3. **They Disagree on the Merits of the Change**

◆ The people initiating the change and those affected by it may be operating with different sets of information or expectations about the reasons for change, the goals and desired outcomes of the change, and the implications of the change.

◆ People may think the proposed change not only won't resolve problems but is also likely to increase them.

4. **They have a Low Personal Tolerance for Change**

◆ Some people just don't tolerate change well.

◆ Attitudes can be difficult to change once they've been learned.

◆ People may feel the need to "save face" because they may have developed or strongly supported the behaviors, practices, or policies that are being changed.

◆ Pressure from friends, family, or neighbors can encourage people to resist change.

Training Instrument 9–10
Personal Plan for Dealing with Change Resistance

Instructions: What actions can you take to reduce change resistance in others? Reflect on the sources of resistance and the actions your small group explored in Training Instrument 9–9 as you develop your plan for reducing resistance to change for your team or workgroup.

Specific actions I will take to reduce change resistance include

1.

2.

3.

4.

5.

6.

Handout 9–5

Why We Value Change Resisters

We value the people who resist change because

- they help clarify the problem that must be addressed by the change

- they identify other problems that may need to be solved first

- they force change leaders to think before they act and implement the change

- their tough questions can strengthen and improve the vision, strategy, and plan for the change

- they let us know who opposes the change and, subsequently, to whom we need to listen and with whom we need to communicate

- they slow down the change, which enables others to more effectively cope with the change

- they may be right, it *is* a dumb idea!

Learning Activity 9-7: Identifying the Perceived Losses and Exploring the Opportunities from a Proposed Change

OBJECTIVES

The objectives of this learning activity are to

- identify the common losses that people perceive they are likely to experience as a result of change

- enable participants to reduce these perceived losses for themselves and others by exploring opportunities created by the change.

MATERIALS

The materials needed for this activity are

- Training Instrument 9–11: Experiencing the Losses of Change

- Training Instrument 9–12: Personal Plan for Action—Dealing with the Perceived Losses

- Handout 9–6: The Crisis of Change

- Flipchart and marking pens

- PowerPoint slides 7–34 through 7–36.

TIME

- 30 minutes

PREPARATIONS

This activity, appropriate for both change leaders and those affected by a change, typically follows Learning Activity 9–6 because the perceived losses of change have an effect on the origin, intensity, and duration of change resistance.

INSTRUCTIONS

1. Display PowerPoint slide 7–34. Suggest that organizational change often presents a crisis for individuals and the entire organization. In-

dicate that the two Chinese characters represent two aspects of the word "crisis."

2. Explain that one of these characters represents "danger." Ask people what they think the second character represents. Someone is likely to offer "opportunity"—agree as you reveal (on the PowerPoint slide) the words "hidden opportunity." Note that, with the crisis of change comes the danger of losing everything, but that along with the danger of losing the safety, security, and comfort of what we have there is also opportunity—opportunity that often reveals itself only when we are compelled to look for it. Hence the hidden opportunity is a partner to the danger presented by a crisis.

3. Suggest that in the midst of the crisis presented by a change, some people only see the danger, while others also are able to see the opportunity that presents itself along with the danger. Note that helping ourselves and others to both see and realize the hidden opportunity is a critical step in dealing with our fears and concerns about a change.

4. Distribute Handout 9–6, indicating that they can use this Chinese script to remind themselves of these two paired outcomes from the crisis often created by change.

5. Distribute Training Instrument 9–11 as you display PowerPoint slide 7–35, which lists the most common perceived losses of change. Indicate that each of these factors is important to people in varying degrees and, when they perceive that the change threatens the loss of one of these factors, they are likely to resist the change.

6. Suggest to participants that helping themselves and others through change involves first understanding which of these common losses is perceived to have the greatest impact and then developing a plan to eliminate, reduce, or offset this loss with a hidden opportunity. Note that, sometimes, simply sharing more information about an impending change and its likely effects can help reduce people's fears and perceptions of danger. Through this sharing of information, they may realize that the change doesn't pose significant loss to them after all. They may even come to understand that there is more that isn't changing than that is changing. In addition to sharing information, however, the plan by the individual, team, depart-

ment, or organization must involve activities that attempt to reduce the perceived loss or provide an offsetting benefit or gain.

7. Ask participants to work by themselves and, thinking of the changes ahead, identify which losses will most concern those affected by the changes (focusing on the left-hand column only at this time). Give them two minutes for this.

8. After a couple of minutes, display PowerPoint slide 7–36 and ask people to work in small groups to, first, discuss the most likely perceived losses from the change and, second, identify two or three actions that people can take to reduce, eliminate, or offset each perceived loss with a hidden opportunity. Ask people to make notes in the space provided to the right of the perceived losses. Give the small groups five to eight minutes for this activity.

9. Reconvene the group and invite individuals to share examples of the most likely perceived losses and their ideas or suggestions for reducing, eliminating, or offsetting these losses with hidden opportunities.

DEBRIEFING

Make the following summary comments as you guide participants in integrating this activity and developing their personal plans for action:

1. Responding effectively to change—for ourselves or helping others—involves making a choice to move past the perceived dangers (by eliminating or reducing the losses) and taking action to realize the hidden opportunities.

2. Perceptions are everything in the world of organizational change, which requires that leaders of a change understand that any leadership or managerial action can be misperceived by others and that these misperceptions can, in turn, lead to the emergence of unwarranted fears. Increasing the frequency and clarity of the communications about the change can help reduce fear and these perceived losses.

3. When change does present a loss to others—or if people still perceive that they will experience a loss—it is up to leaders of the change and those negatively affected by the change to take direct action to offset the loss with a gain. This involves searching for sometimes creative solutions that address the underlying losses, fears, and concerns.

4. Not all losses can be eliminated and not all people are able to see the hidden opportunity buried within a change. Although change leaders need to do their best to understand and reduce the real losses people experience, there will be times when the organization—and individuals—simply need to move on.

5. Refer to the earlier comment that change is inevitable, growth is optional (PowerPoint slide 7–29) and suggest that moving beyond the pain of change and realizing the hidden opportunities are fundamentally a personal choice. Although the organization and its leaders can help people through this process, they still must make this journey themselves—from Fear, Anger, and Resistance through Inquiry, Experimentation, and Discovery and toward Learning, Acceptance, and Commitment (all stages of the emotional journey people take through change; see Learning Activity 9–2).

6. Direct participants to Training Instrument 9–12: Personal Plan for Action: Dealing with the Perceived Losses. Ask them to spend the next five minutes identifying, first, some specific losses that people perceive they are likely to experience from the change and, second, specific actions that they will take to eliminate or reduce the loss, or offset the perceived losses of a coming change. Ask them to identify any additional opportunities that the change may present and to identify specific actions that they and others in their area can take to help realize the opportunity.

7. As time permits, ask each participant to pair up with another person at the table to share their personal plans. Encourage the pairs to help each other strengthen their personal plans by offering additional strategies and ideas.

Training Instrument 9–11
The Perceived Losses of Change

1. What are the most likely losses that people *perceive* they will experience from the changes the organization is undergoing?

2. How can we help ourselves and others overcome these perceived losses? Offset them with a gain or opportunity?

❶ THE PERCEIVED LOSSES OF CHANGE	❷ RESPONDING TO THE PERCEIVED LOSSES
1. **Job Security**—People may fear job loss or a loss of financial resources due to a reduction in their job or income level.	
2. **Psychological Comfort or Security**—People want to feel safe, secure, and comfortable. They may perceive that the change threatens their level of safety, comfort, security, and self-confidence by reducing their level of certainty about the world around them.	
3. **Control over One's Future**—Related to the perceived loss of psychological comfort or security, people may perceive that the change threatens their ability to control their future actions, decisions, and identity.	
4. **Purpose or Meaning**—People may perceive that their fundamental purpose and meaning in life is jeopardized. Change, they believe, threatens to take away the identities, hopes, and aspirations that make their lives meaningful.	
5. **Competence**—People may believe that the change will reduce their ability to do their work or jobs well. They may feel unprepared for new responsibilities and duties, which can lead to embarrassment and a reduction in self-confidence.	
6. **Social Connections**—People may believe that their social contacts with customers, co-workers, or managers will disappear. This can result in a loss in their sense of belonging to a team, group, or	

continued on next page

Training Instrument 9–11, continued

The Perceived Losses of Change

❶ THE PERCEIVED LOSSES OF CHANGE	❷ RESPONDING TO THE PERCEIVED LOSSES
the organization. Since so much of our sense of self evolves through our relationships to others, this perceived loss tends to be the most traumatic.	
7. *Territory*—People believe they may lose a sense of certainty about the territory or area that used to be theirs. This territory includes physical workspace, expertise, job titles, assignments, and psychological space.	
8. *Future Opportunities*—When a change threatens expected rewards and opportunities, people fear they may lose a deserved reward that they have worked hard to achieve.	
9. *Power*—Change can threaten a person's sense of power and influence in their organization and life. People may perceive that the change takes away part of what enables them to feel effective.	
10. *Social Status*—People may perceive that the change will erode the status that they have achieved (through competence, influence, or hard work) compared to other people. They fear that what they have worked hard to accomplish may disappear.	
11. *Trust in Others*—People may lose their trust and faith in others—especially leaders and others whom they have admired in the past—when the impending change threatens to take away other things of value.	
12. *Independence and Autonomy*—When change is introduced, the perceived loss of competence creates a related secondary loss of independence and autonomy, in which people perceive that their ability to be self-directed and self-managed will be eroded.	

Training Instrument 9–12

Personal Plan for Action: Dealing with the Perceived Losses

Instructions: In the columns and spaces below, answer the following questions.

1. What are the greatest perceived losses that people may experience as a result of the changes facing the organization? How can you and others eliminate, reduce, or offset these perceived losses? How can you help yourself and others realize the "hidden opportunities" from the change?

THE GREATEST PERCEIVED LOSSES FOR MY TEAM/WORK AREA...	ACTIONS TO ELIMINATE OR REDUCE THE LOSS OR OFFSET THE LOSS WITH A HIDDEN OPPORTUNITY...

2. What additional hidden opportunities are presented by the change? Identify at least one hidden opportunity and the actions that you and others can take to help realize this opportunity.

HIDDEN OPPORTUNITY...	ACTIONS TO REALIZE OR ACHIEVE THE OPPORTUNITY...

Handout 9–6
The Crisis of Change

 **Danger!**

 **Hidden Opportunity**

Learning Activity 9–8: Strengthening Change Resilience

OBJECTIVES

The objectives of this learning activity are to

- identify the characteristics that enable people to deal most effectively with change

- guide participants in developing a personal plan for strengthening resilience in themselves and others.

MATERIALS

- Training Instrument 9–13: Characteristics of Change Resilience

- Training Instrument 9–14: Personal Plan for Strengthening Resilience in Others

- Training Instrument 9–15: Personal Plan for Strengthening Your Resilience

- Handout 9–7: Human Nature and the Character of Change

- Flipchart and marking pens

- PowerPoint slides 7–37 through 7–41.

TIME

- 35 minutes

PREPARATIONS

This activity immediately follows Learning Activity 9–7.

- Create a blank flipchart page titled "Developing and Strengthening Resilience in Others."

INSTRUCTIONS

1. Point out to participants that, throughout this change training session, you have discussed the variety of reasons why people sometimes have a difficult time dealing with the changes in their lives. In-

dicate that you have explored the sources of resistance to change, including the perceived losses of change.

2. Suggest that there is another reason that change creates stress for people. By its very nature because it breaks from the familiar, change disrupts the capacity to envision oneself in the future; it alters the ability to feel secure and confident that one has a place and about the roles one plays in the world after the change has occurred.

3. Distribute Handout 9–7 and display PowerPoint slide 7–37. Note that a key characteristic of human nature is our desire to maintain control over the events and circumstances of our lives. Guide participants through the points on this slide, noting that satisfying the need for control gives a sense of stability, security, and self-confidence.

4. When change disrupts one's ability to maintain control over one's life, the result is disorientation, anxiety, fear, confusion, and insecurity. And the greater the degree to which a given change disrupts the sense of control, the higher the levels of confusion, frustration, and insecurity one is likely to experience.

5. People tend to feel anxious and frightened when they can't see a clear picture of themselves in the future or when what they expect to happen doesn't happen.

6. Add that not all people, however, end up feeling insecure, anxious, and fearful in the face of disruptive change. Note that studies of children successfully coping with the challenges of inner-city life, families remaining healthy despite experiencing crisis, and the frail elderly who outlive their peers suggest that there is a personal characteristic that people can develop in themselves that can strengthen their response to change and stress. This quality is called *resilience.*

7. Display PowerPoint slide 7–38 as you note that Webster's dictionary defines resilience as "an ability to recover from or adjust easily to misfortune or change." Another definition includes "the capability of a strained body to recover its size and shape" after being subjected to adversity or stress.

8. Suggest that individuals have different levels of resilience and that their respective resiliency determines, to a significant extent, whether they view change as a threat (danger) or an opportunity. Cultivating

and reinforcing resiliency in oneself and others reduces the negative effects of change (by shifting the focus toward the hidden opportunities) and smoothes its acceptance.

9. Distribute Training Instrument 9–13 and display PowerPoint slide 7–39. Note that these personal characteristics compose the quality of resilience. When these characteristics are developed, strengthened, and reinforced, the research suggests that people are more likely to remain healthy and strong as they move through change (Bernard, 1991; Connor, 1992; Walsh, 1998).

10. The research also reveals that developing resilience is a shared responsibility between the individual and the environment. This suggests that people can take steps to strengthen their own resilience and that organizational leaders can help develop resilience in others by encouraging and reinforcing its emergence.

11. Invite participants to review the qualities of resilience on their own, making notes in the margins about their thoughts on how their organization could help develop and strengthen resilience in employees at all levels. Ask them to identify any questions they may have about any of these characteristics or the quality of resilience itself. Give participants about three minutes to review the resilience characteristics.

12. Display PowerPoint slide 7–40 and direct participants to work in small groups to, first, discuss their reactions to and questions about the concept of resilience and its dimensions and, second, suggest three to four specific actions that organizational leaders and individuals can take to develop and strengthen resilience in themselves and others. Encourage them to explore and try to answer any of their questions about resilience and its component dimensions. Give the small groups approximately eight minutes for this discussion.

13. After about eight minutes, invite the small groups to share their reactions to the concept of resilience and explore answers to their questions. Then draw out the actions that organizational leaders and others can take to develop and strengthen resilience in themselves and others. If desired, record the suggestions on the prepared flipchart.

DEBRIEFING

Make the following summary, integrating comments on resilience as you guide them toward developing their personal plans:

1. Display PowerPoint slide 7–41, noting the quote by Dr. Michael McGriffy. Suggest that the more we can bend with the winds of change—while staying true to ourselves (a blade of grass still stays a blade of grass, despite the wind)—the more likely we can stay healthy over the long term.

2. Personal resilience is an important internal human mechanism that, if developed, enables someone to successfully cope—in many cases even thrive—in the midst of the stress and turmoil of change. By developing or strengthening these resilience characteristics in themselves, people are able to restore a level of control and certainty in their lives that a change may have jeopardized.

3. People who are resilient have the capacity to see the hidden opportunity in any crisis that change creates and, although they might prefer that the change weren't happening, they accept that change of some sort is inevitable.

4. Resilient people make efforts to actively shape change to ensure that, at some level, it responds to their own needs and the needs of others. Resilient people may disagree with a change, but, when change is inevitable, they recognize this and work hard to make it work on terms that respond to both the forces for change and their own preferences.

5. Reiterate that both individuals and organizational leaders play key roles in developing and strengthening resilience; that individuals must cultivate this quality in themselves and leaders must take actions that encourage its development.

For leader/manager/supervisor training:

Direct participants to Training Instrument 9–14: Personal Plan for Strengthening Resilience in Others. Ask them to spend the next five minutes identifying some specific actions they will take as a leader or manager to develop and strengthen resilience in employees. Encourage them to reflect upon the recent small-group discussion on organizational actions to develop resilience. Ask them to identify at least three actions that they can take to help develop and strengthen resilience in others. As time permits, ask participants to pair up with another person at their table to share their personal plan. Encourage the pairs to help each other strengthen their personal plans by offering additional resilience development strategies.

For employee training:

Direct participants to Training Instrument 9–15: Personal Plan for Strengthening Your Resilience. Ask them to spend the next five minutes identifying at least three specific actions that they will take to develop and strengthen their own resilience. As time permits, ask each participant to pair up with another person at the table to share their personal plans. Encourage the pairs to help each other strengthen their personal plans by offering additional resilience development strategies.

Training Instrument 9–13

Characteristics of Resilience

Instructions: Read and consider the descriptions of characteristics of resilience in the left-hand column below. In the right-hand column, list several ways you might develop each of the characteristics.

PERSONAL RESILIENCE DIMENSION	IDEAS TO DEVELOP THIS DIMENSION
1. *Self-assurance:* Display a sense of security and self-assurance that acknowledges that life is complex and challenging but filled with opportunity. Develop a positive outlook about yourself, your work unit or team, the organization, and life in general.	
2. *Clarity of personal vision:* Develop a clear vision of what you want to achieve, accomplish, or create and where you want to go in your job, career, and life.	
3. *Flexibility:* Demonstrate adaptability and flexibility in the face of uncertainty and stress. Accept the need to shift and redefine (if necessary) your direction, focus, and vision as you learn new information from the environment, peers, customers, family, and other sources.	
4. *Organizational skills:* Develop personalized methods, structures, and systems for organizing and managing confusion, chaos, and ambiguity. Develop stable structures to ride out a turbulent storm. If necessary, focus on one day, one week, or one project at a time.	
5. *Problem-solving skills:* Develop the capacity to effectively think through	

continued on next page

Training Instrument 9–13, continued
Characteristics of Resilience

PERSONAL RESILIENCE DIMENSION	IDEAS TO DEVELOP THIS DIMENSION
and resolve personal and professional problems. See problems as challenges and opportunities. Fine-tune your skills in collaborating with others and doing critical, systemic, and creative out-of-the-box thinking.	
6. *Interpersonal competence:* Demonstrate responsiveness, empathy, and caring for others. This quality also involves communicating effectively with others and displaying a sense of humor—an ability to laugh at yourself.	
7. *Social connections:* Build bridges and form partnerships with the people around you. Work with others to discover ways to make sense of the changing environment. Share ideas, solutions, problems, frustrations, opportunities, and accomplishments. Focus on discovering areas of common ground and answers to common problems.	
8. *Proactive approach:* Engage change directly rather than denying, fighting, or working against it. Accept that change is inevitable, but growth is optional, and find a way to make change work *for* you. Focus on what *you* can do, not on what others are doing to you.	

Training Instrument 9–14
Personal Plan for Strengthening Resilience in Others

Developing resilience is a shared responsibility of the individual and the environment or organization. Because both have a role to play in developing and strengthening resilience, change leaders have a responsibility to support and reinforce others' efforts in becoming more resilient.

Instructions: Consider what actions you can take as a leader, manager, or supervisor to help develop and strengthen the resilience of those in your work area, and how you can reinforce and support their resilience-building efforts. Refer to the ideas and suggestions shared in this workshop during the discussion of Training Instrument 9–13 (Characteristics of Resilience). In the numbered spaces below, identify your plan for helping others develop and strengthen their resilience. Answer these questions: What actions will you take? Who needs the greatest assistance? Where can you be most helpful to others in building resilience?

1.

2.

3.

4.

5.

6.

Training Instrument 9–15
Personal Plan for Strengthening Your Resilience

Instructions: Reflect on the dimensions of resilience as noted in Training Instrument 9–13. Which dimensions are already well developed for you? Which dimensions could you work at strengthening? Identify the specific things you can do to develop and strengthen your own resilience. In the numbered spaces below, identify your next steps for developing and strengthening your resilience.

1.

2.

3.

4.

5.

6.

Now identify how your supervisor can help you develop and strengthen your resilience.

1.

2.

3.

4.

Handout 9–7
Human Nature and the Character of Change

There are certain characteristics of being human that pose a special challenge when change—especially radical or traumatic change—occurs:

♦ People find comfort in being able to maintain control over the events and circumstances of their lives. The most basic and fundamental level in Abraham Maslow's hierarchy of needs represents this core characteristic of human nature. Satisfying this basic need gives people a sense of stability, security, and safety.

♦ With this basic need met, people develop self-confidence and psychological health and integration by building stable and effective relationships with others.

♦ Much of our sense of control, comfort, and psychological well-being results from the degree of certainty we have about the path of our lives. When our experience matches our own expectations about our future, we feel a measure of control and certainty. [6]

♦ The challenge that change presents is that it disrupts our ability to predict with certainty what's in store for us tomorrow. When change threatens our capacity to envision our own future, when it seems to jeopardize our future safety and security, and when it jeopardizes our relationships with others, we can be plunged into insecurity, self-doubt, confusion, fear, anxiety, and even depression.

♦ The more a given change or set of changes disrupts our sense of self and our ability to envision our future with a degree of certainty, the more confusion, fear, anxiety, and self-doubt we are likely to experience.

When people first hear of an approaching change, they want to see a clear picture of it and they want to see where they will fit into that picture in the future. Therefore, when changes are introduced—especially changes that radically alter someone's ability to envision his or her future role—change leaders must work hard to help people see themselves in the future, to restore some sense of continuity and certainty. Although the new level of continuity and certainty that leaders help people create may never approximate what people once had, it at least gives them a sense of direction, focus, stability, and order.

What to Do Next

- ◆ Decide where and with whom you will begin your leading change training program.

- ◆ Start designing your leading change workshop programs.

◆ ◆ ◆

The next chapter provides a number of training tools that you will find helpful in facilitating and evaluating your leading change workshops.

Training Tools

- Seven training tools to support and enhance the learning environment

This chapter presents training tools to help you create an environment that supports learning. Although the use of any of these tools is optional, we believe that effective trainers use tools like these to facilitate learning.

Training Tool 10–1:
Training Room Configuration/Layout

Training room configuration and layout play a critical role in facilitating learning. The way you organize participants' seating influences their focus during the session—toward the trainer or their fellow participants, or both—and helps set expectations for interaction or involvement. Tool 10–1 offers a training room configuration that the authors have found to be most conducive to learning.

Tool 10-1

Training Room Configuration/Layout

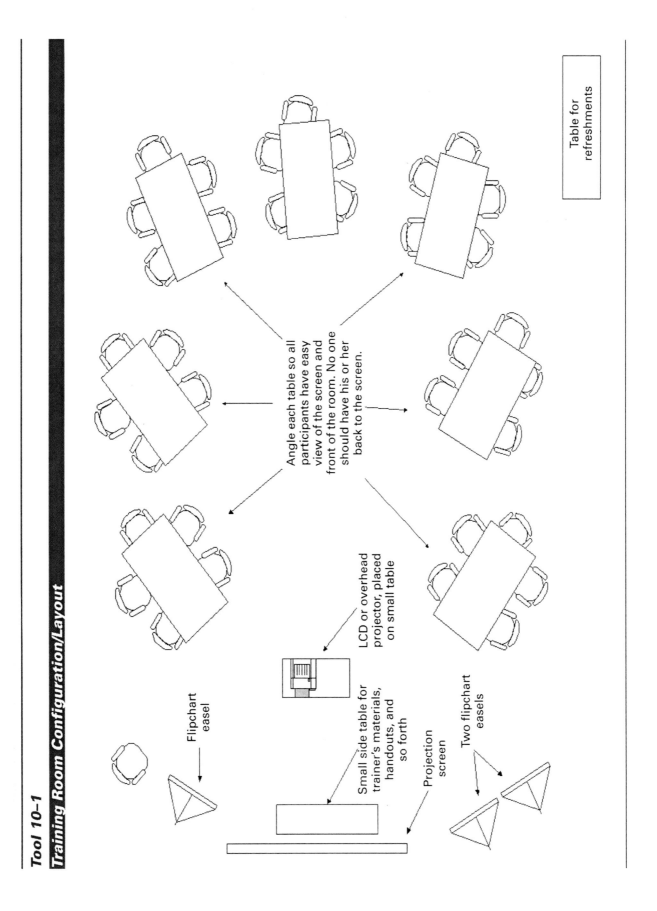

Angle each table so all participants have easy view of the screen and front of the room. No one should have his or her back to the screen.

Table for refreshments

Flipchart easel

LCD or overhead projector, placed on small table

Small side table for trainer's materials, handouts, and so forth

Projection screen

Two flipchart easels

Training Tool 10–2:
Ah Ha! Sheet

The Ah Ha! Sheet is a simple tool to help focus the learning of participants. During the training day participants are immersed in a wide variety of new ideas, models, methods, and strategies. Some of these ideas will easily stick and become part of the participants' new consciousness. Others, however—no matter how useful or relevant—can too easily be lost as the learner attempts to put new knowledge and skills into practice. If participants use the Ah Ha! Sheet to recognize and record significant learning moments, ideas, methods, and strategies—in their own words—they are more likely to retain their learning. The Ah Ha! Sheet also serves as an after-the-training memory jogger that reminds participants of key learning points from the session.

Tool 10–2

Ah Ha! Sheet

Instructions: Jot down the most significant insights, perspectives, and practical ideas that you pick up from this seminar. These Ah Ha's are the ideas, tools, methods, and approaches that you are most likely to remember and put into practice when you return to work. Identify the ideas that will help you transfer your learning from this session to your workplace.

1.

2.

3.

4.

5.

6.

7.

8.

9.

10.

Training Tool 10–3: Goal-Setting Worksheet

Having participants set specific learning goals and objectives for the Leading Change Workshop is an essential step that focuses their energy and attention on achieving meaningful results. Research into both goal setting and the Expectancy Theory of motivation suggests that people will have more commitment to achieving a goal (in this case a learning objective) if they are involved in developing a specific goal for themselves. Further, the expectancy theory of motivation (Vroom, 1964; Porter and Lawler, 1968) suggests that motivation to achieve a goal is enhanced by the answers to three questions:

1. If I try to achieve a specific goal, will I be successful?

2. If I am successful in achieving the goal, what are the outcomes I am likely to receive?

3. How important are these outcomes?

The participant goal-setting worksheet attempts to increase participants' motivation to learn by asking them to identify a specific goal for themselves, identify the rewards or outcomes they are likely to realize if they achieve that learning objective, and identify how important this reward or outcome is to them. These three questions help target the participants' attention on learning in order to help them increase the likelihood of realizing a reward or outcome that they value highly.

Tool 10–3
Goal-Setting Worksheet

1. **Learning Objective:** What do I want to learn or what behavior do I want to change as a result of this course?

    _____

    _____

    _____

    _____

    _____

    _____

    To what degree do I believe that this program will help me achieve this objective?

    Not at all ☐   ☐   ☐   ☐   ☐   ☐ Quite a bit
               1   2   3   4   5   6

2. **Outcomes from Achieving My Learning Objective:** What are the potential rewards or outcomes that I expect to get if I achieve my objective?

    _____

    _____

    _____

    _____

    _____

    _____

    To what degree do I believe that achieving my objective will bring about this outcome?

    Not at all ☐   ☐   ☐   ☐   ☐   ☐ Quite a bit
               1   2   3   4   5   6

3. **Value of This Reward:** How valuable is this reward? To what degree do I value this outcome or reward?

    Not at all ☐   ☐   ☐   ☐   ☐   ☐ Quite a bit
               1   2   3   4   5   6

Training Tool 10–4:
Sample Training Program Evaluation

Evaluating the effectiveness of your training program provides you with an opportunity to

◆ measure the impact that the training has had on participant learning and behavior and organizational results

◆ gather ideas for improving or enhancing the workshop for future sessions.

There are many variations of training program design, and we encourage you to review the training evaluation literature and resources to develop your own or use what others have developed. In the book *The Winning Trainer* (1996), Julius Eitington offers a variety of training evaluation tools, emphasizing those that actively involve the participants. Included in the chapter titled "Using Participative Methods to Evaluate Training" are both quantitative methods (the reaction sheet) and post-training assessments of learning and behavior change.

Two other useful resources are *ASTD Trainer's Toolkit: Evaluation Instruments* and *ASTD Trainer's Toolkit: More Evaluation Instruments*. Both books offer a variety of training evaluation forms used by organizations throughout the United States and include articles from *Training & Development* magazine.

ASTD's annual "Learning Outcomes Report" highlights the results of efforts to measure organizational investments in education and training. The report includes multiple training evaluation forms (reaction sheets and follow-up assessments) that were used in the research. Interested organizations can also participate in ASTD's ongoing research on this topic by becoming part of the annual study of learning outcomes. The report is available in .pdf format for download by ASTD members at the research section of the ASTD Website.

Regardless of the format or structure you use to evaluate your training program and its learning outcomes, there are a number of key questions that you should include in your assessment efforts.

Tool 10–4
Sample Training Program Evaluation

Instructions: Your training program reaction sheet should address at least some of the following dimensions of participants' learning experience. Participants are asked to read each statement and respond using this 6-point "agree" scale:

1 = STRONGLY DISAGREE   4 = SLIGHTLY AGREE

2 = DISAGREE   5 = AGREE

3 = SLIGHTLY DISAGREE   6 = STRONGLY AGREE

Logistics or Administrative Topics:

_____ **1.** The pre-session information about the workshop provided useful information on the workshop's learning objectives and desired outcomes.

_____ **2.** The training room was arranged so that it facilitated my learning.

_____ **3.** The training room temperature was comfortable throughout the session.

_____ **4.** I had the knowledge or skills required to effectively participate in this workshop.

Workshop Content:

_____ **5.** The workshop's learning objectives were clearly defined.

_____ **6.** This workshop was timely and relevant—it dealt with an issue with which I am currently dealing.

_____ **7.** This workshop provided practical and useful knowledge and skills that are immediately applicable to my job.

_____ **8.** This workshop provided me new information, ideas, methods, and techniques.

_____ **9.** This workshop helped me achieve my personal learning objectives for this topic.

Workshop Design:

_____ **10.** The participant materials (such as handouts, workbooks, cases) were useful throughout the workshop.

_____ **11.** The way that this workshop was delivered was an effective way for me to learn this topic.

_____ **12.** I had enough time to understand, learn, and integrate the workshop materials.

_____ **13.** The workshop content was logically organized.

_____ **14.** There was a good mix of teaching methods, formats, and audiovisuals that enabled me to learn the course content.

continued on next page

Tool 10–4, continued

Sample Training Program Evaluation

Trainer or Workshop Instructor:

_____15. The instructor was knowledgeable in the workshop subject.

_____16. The instructor was organized and prepared.

_____17. The instructor established a good learning environment.

_____18. The instructor was open to participants' questions and concerns and was willing to adjust the program to meet participants' needs.

_____19. The instructor generated active discussion and involvement by participants.

_____20. Overall, I was satisfied with the instructor.

Overall Assessment:

21. Overall, the pace of this workshop was *[circle one]:*

　　　　　　　Too fast　　　　　　Too slow　　　　　　Just right

22. This workshop *[circle one]:*

　　　　　　Did not meet　　　　Met my　　　　　Exceeded my
　　　　　　my expectations　　expectations　　expectations

23. My overall evaluation of this workshop is *[check one box]:*

Very　☐　☐　☐　☐　☐　☐　☐　☐　☐　☐　Excellent
Poor　1　2　3　4　5　6　7　8　9　10

Comments:

24. What I found most helpful from this workshop was . . .

25. Ideas for improving or strengthening this workshop include . . .

26. Additional comments:

Training Tool 10–5: The Parking Lot

Throughout many training workshops—and perhaps especially in workshops dealing with a specific organizational change—issues and questions often arise that either the trainer or participants are unable to address or do not have time to address. The Parking Lot can be a place to "park" ideas and questions for a future discussion. Also known as an Issues Bin or Future File, the Parking Lot can be a useful tool for recognizing the value of a question or concern by recording it on a flipchart page. The Parking Lot can be revisited later in the training session, either in a follow-up session (once answers are gathered) or in communications with participants following the session.

The usefulness of the Parking Lot lies in its ability to honor the concerns and questions participants bring to the session while avoiding distracting the session with things that are either off-target for the session or that can't be addressed by the people in the room. The Parking Lot is particularly helpful in bringing to the surface issues that must be addressed by change leaders.

Training Tool 10–6:
The Question Board

Similar to the Parking Lot, the Question Board is simply a flipchart page depicting a large question mark within a square. Each participant table should have at least one pack of sticky notes. At any time during the session, a participant with a question or concern writes it on a note and places the note on the page within the square. Individuals can post questions or concerns at breaks or any time they want.

The trainer or facilitator monitors the Question Board and—when he or she deems it appropriate—reads the question or concern to the group and either answers the question or facilitates a group discussion. After a question or concern has been addressed, this is indicated by placing the sticky note outside the square.

Any questions or concerns remaining at the end of the workshop can be addressed in the conclusion of the session or highlighted as an issue for future consideration or follow-up.

Training Tool 10–7: Selecting Group Leaders

When you ask participants to "discuss this in your small groups," it is useful to have the group select a discussion or group leader. Leaders help focus the energy of the group and help create some accountability for the assigned task. It's also a good idea to encourage the rotation of leadership among the group members to distribute participation and responsibility.

Some ideas for selecting and rotating group leaders include

- ◆ the person with the first or last birthday in the year

- ◆ the person with the most uncommon middle name

- ◆ the person who had the farthest or shortest distance to travel from his or her home to attend the workshop

- ◆ the person with the shortest or longest hair

- ◆ the person to the right or left of the last discussion leader

- ◆ the most or least senior person in terms of years with the organization.

Using the Compact Disc

Insert the CD and locate the file *How to Use This CD.txt.*

Contents of the CD

The compact disc that accompanies this workbook on new employee orientation contains three types of files. All of the files can be used on a variety of computer platforms.

- **Adobe .pdf documents.** These include handouts and training tools.

- **Microsoft PowerPoint presentations.** These presentations add interest and depth to several training activities included in the workbook.

- **Microsoft PowerPoint files of overhead transparency masters.** This file makes it easy to print viewgraphs and handouts in black-and-white rather than using an office copier. They contain only text and line drawings; there are no images to print in grayscale.

Computer Requirements

To read or print the .pdf files on the CD, you must have Adobe Acrobat Reader software installed on your system. The program can be downloaded free of cost from the Adobe Website, *www.adobe.com.*

To use or adapt the contents of the PowerPoint presentation files on the CD, you must have Microsoft PowerPoint software installed on your system. If you simply want to view the PowerPoint documents, you must have an appropriate viewer installed on your system. Microsoft provides various viewers free for downloading from its Website, *www.microsoft.com.*

Printing from the CD

TEXT FILES

You can print the assessments and handouts using Adobe Acrobat Reader. Simply open the .pdf file and print as many copies as you need. The following documents can be directly printed from the CD:

- Training Instrument 6–1: Characteristics of and Leader Actions for Each Phase in the Change Journey

- Training Instrument 7–1: Reflections on Leading Change

- Training Instrument 7–2: Next Steps for Leading Change

- Training Instrument 9–1: Perceptions of Change

- Training Instrument 9–2: Experiencing Personal Change

- Training Instrument 9–3: Characteristics of and Actions for Each Phase of the Change Journey

- Training Instrument 9–4: Personal Plan for Helping Yourself and Others through Change

- Training Instrument 9–5: Introducing, Leading, and Sustaining Commitment to a Change

- Training Instrument 9–6: Personal Plan for Initiating and Sustaining a Change

- Training Instrument 9–7: The Forces Driving Change

- Training Instrument 9–8: Responding to the Forces of Change

- Training Instrument 9–9: The Origins of Change Resistance

- Training Instrument 9–10: Personal Plan for Dealing with Change Resistance

- Training Instrument 9–11: The Preceived Losses of Change

- Training Instrument 9–12: Personal Plan for Action: Dealing with the Perceived Losses

- Training Instrument 9–13: Characteristics of Resilience

- Training Instrument 9–14: Personal Plan for Strengthening Resilience in Others

- Training Instrument 9–15: Personal Plan for Strengthening Your Resilience

- Handout 6–1: Components of a Change Implementation Plan

- Handout 9–1: The Journey through Change

- Handout 9–2: Actions for Guiding People through Change

- Handout 9–3: An Integrated Model for Leading Change

- Handout 9–4: Actions for Introducing and Leading Change

- Handout 9–5: Why We Value Change Resisters

- Handout 9–6: The Crisis of Change

- Handout 9–7: Human Nature and the Character of Change

- Tool 10–1: Training Room Configuration/Layout

- Tool 10–2: Ah Ha! Sheet

- Tool 10–3: Goal-Setting Worksheet

- Tool 10–4: Sample Training Program Evaluation

POWERPOINT SLIDES

You can print the presentation slides directly from this CD using Microsoft PowerPoint. Simply open the .ppt files and print as many copies as you need. You can also make handouts of the presentations by printing 2, 4, or 6 "slides" per page. These slides will be in color, with design elements embedded. PowerPoint also permits you to print these in grayscale or black-and-white, although printing from the overhead masters file will yield better black-and-white representations. Many trainers who use personal computers to project their presentations bring along viewgraphs, just in case there are glitches in the system.

Table A–1

Navigating Through a PowerPoint Presentation

KEY	POWERPOINT "SHOW" ACTION
Space bar *or* Enter *or* Mouse click	Advance through custom animations embedded in the presentation
Backspace	Back up to the last projected element of the presentation
Escape	Abort the presentation
B *or* b	Blank the screen to black
B *or* b *(repeat)*	Resume the presentation
W *or* w	Blank the screen to white
W *or* w *(repeat)*	Resume the presentation

Adapting the PowerPoint Slides

You can modify or otherwise customize the slides by opening and editing them in the appropriate application. However, you must retain the denotation of the original source of the material—it is illegal to pass it off as your own work. You may indicate that a document was adapted from this workbook, written and copyrighted by Jeffrey Russell and Linda Russell and published by ASTD. The files will open as "Read Only," so before you adapt them you will need to save them onto your hard drive under a different filename.

Showing the PowerPoint Presentations

On the CD, the following PowerPoint presentations are included:

- Executive Briefing.ppt

- Leading Change–Managers.ppt

- Leading Change–Employees.ppt

- Follow-Up (Managers).ppt

- Follow-Up (Employees).ppt

Having the presentations in .ppt format means that it automatically shows full-screen when you double-click on its filename. You also can open Microsoft PowerPoint and launch it from there.

Use the space bar, the enter key, or mouse clicks to advance through a show. Press the backspace key to back up. Use the escape key to abort a presentation. If you want to blank the screen to black while the group discusses a point, press the B key. Pressing it again restores the show. If you want to blank the screen to a white background, do the same with the W key. Table A–1 summarizes these instructions.

We strongly recommend that trainers practice making presentations before using them in training situations. You should be confident that you can cogently expand on the points featured in the presentations and discuss the methods for working through them. If you want to engage your training participants fully (rather than worrying about how to show the next slide), become familiar with this simple technology *before* you need to use it. A good practice is to insert notes into the *Speaker's Notes* feature of the PowerPoint program, print them out, and have them in front of you when you present the slides.

For Further Reading

ADULT LEARNING AND TRAINING PROGRAM DESIGN/EVALUATION

ASTD Trainer's Toolkit: Evaluation Instruments. Alexandria, VA: American Society for Training & Development, 1991.

Broad, Mary, and John Newstrom. *Transfer of Training.* Reading, MA: Addison-Wesley, 1992.

Brookfield, Stephen D. *Understanding and Facilitating Adult Learning.* San Francisco: Jossey-Bass, 1991.

Eitington, Julius E. *The Winning Trainer* (3rd edition). Houston: Gulf Publishing, 1996.

Kirkpatrick, Donald L. "Techniques for Evaluating Training Programs," a four-part series that began in the November 1959 issue of the *Journal for the American Society for Training Directors* (now *Training & Development*).

Kirkpatrick, Donald L. *Evaluating Training Programs: The Four Levels* (2nd edition). San Francisco: Berrett-Koehler, 1998.

Markova, Dawna. *The Art of the Possible.* York Beach, ME: Conari Press, 1991.

Phillips, Jack J. *Return on Investment in Training and Performance Improvement Programs: A Step-By-Step Manual for Calculating the Financial Return on Investment.* Burlington, MA: Butterworth-Heinemann, 1997.

Renner, Peter Franz. *The Instructor's Survival Kit: A Handbook for Teachers and Adults* (2nd edition). Vancouver, BC: Training Associates, Ltd., 1989.

Russell, Lou. *The Accelerated Learning Fieldbook*. San Francisco: Jossey-Bass/Pfeiffer, 1999.

Schwarz, Roger. *The Skilled Facilitator: Practical Wisdom for Developing Effective Groups*. San Francisco: Jossey-Bass, 1994.

Stadius, Ruth, ed. *ASTD Trainer's Toolkit: More Evaluation Instruments*. Alexandria, VA: American Society for Training & Development, 1999.

LEADING CHANGE

Bridges, William. *Managing Transitions*. Reading, MA: Addison-Wesley, 1991.

Conner, Daryl R. *Managing at the Speed of Change*. New York: Villard Books, Random House, 1992.

Katzenbach, Jon R., Frederick Beckett, Steven Dichter, Marc Feigen, Christopher Gagnon, Quentin Hope, and Timothy Ling. *Real Change Leaders: How You Can Create Growth and High Performance at Your Company*. New York: Times Books, 1995.

Kissler, Gary D. *The Change Riders*. Reading, MA: Addison-Wesley, 1991.

Lewin, Kurt. *Field Theory in Social Science*. New York: Harper & Row, 1951.

Quinn, Robert E. *Deep Change: Discovering the Leader Within*. San Francisco: Jossey-Bass, 1996.

Russell, Jeffrey, and Linda Russell. *Managing Change*. Dubuque, IA: Kendall/Hunt, 1998.

RESILIENCE

Bernard, Bonnie. *Fostering Resiliency in Kids*. Portland, OR: Northwest Regional Education Laboratory, 1991. Available at http://www.wested.org/cs/wew/view/rs/93.

Walsh, Froma. *Strengthening Family Resilience*. New York: Gilford Press, 1998.

EXPECTANCY THEORY OF MOTIVATION

Porter, L. W., and E. E. Lawler. *Managerial Attitudes and Performance*. Homewood, IL: Irwin-Dorsey, 1968.

Vroom, V. H. *Work and Motivation*. New York: John Wiley, 1964.

Jeffrey and Linda Russell are the founders and co-directors of Russell Consulting, Inc., headquartered in Madison, Wisconsin (www.RussellConsultingInc.com). For more than 15 years Jeff and Linda have provided consulting and training services in such areas as leadership, strategic thinking and planning, change implementation, employee quality of worklife surveys, organizational development, performance coaching, and performance management. Their diverse list of clients includes *Fortune* 500 companies, small businesses, social or nonprofit organizations, and government agencies.

Jeff has a bachelor of arts degree in humanism and cultural change and a master of arts in industrial relations, both from the University of Wisconsin. He serves as an ad hoc faculty member for the University of Wisconsin, teaching for the Small Business Development Center, the Wisconsin Certified Public Manager Program, and a number of other certification programs with the University of Wisconsin campuses. Jeff is a frequent presenter at local, state, regional, and international conferences.

Linda has a bachelor of arts degree in social work and completed graduate work in rehabilitation counseling. She specializes in designing and implementing quality of worklife surveys and in facilitating team and organizational development interventions.

Jeff and Linda have written three other books, including *Managing Change* (1998), and publish a journal of tips for leading organizations, *Workplace Enhancement Notes*.

With a company vision of helping to create and sustain great organizations, Russell Consulting, Inc., integrates theory, research, and "real-world" experience in their daily consulting and training practice. Jeff and Linda help their clients find practical management solutions to a challenging world that too often offers strategies that are long on hype and short on substance.